PENGUIN BOOKS

THE INVENTION OF SOLITUDE

PAUL AUSTER is the author of the novels *The Brooklyn Follies*, *Oracle Night*, *The Book of Illusions*, *Timbuktu*, *Mr. Vertigo*, *Leviathan* (awarded the 1993 Prix Médicis Étranger), *The Music of Chance* (nominated for the 1991 PEN/Faulkner Award), *Moon Palace*, *In the Country of Last Things*, and the three novels known as "The New York Trilogy": *City of Glass*, *Ghosts*, and *The Locked Room*. He has also written two memoirs (*The Invention of Solitude* and *Hand to Mouth*), a collection of essays, and a volume of poems, and edited the book *I Thought My Father Was God: And Other True Tales from NPR's National Story Project*. Auster was the recipient of the 2006 Prince of Asturias Award for Letters and was inducted into the American Academy of Arts and Letters in 2006. He has won literary fellowships from the National Endowment for the Arts in both poetry and prose, and in 1990 received the Morton Dauwen Zabel Award from the American Academy and Institute of Arts and Letters. He wrote the screenplays for *Smoke*, *Blue in the Face*, and *Lulu on the Bridge*, which he also directed. His work has been translated into more than thirty languages. He lives in Brooklyn, New York.

PASCAL BRUCKNER, an essayist and novelist, is the author of *Evil Angles*, *The Tears of the White Man: Compassion as Contempt*, and *The Temptation of Innocence: Living in the Age of Entitlement*. He lives in Paris.

PAUL AUSTER

THE INVENTION
of SOLITUDE

Introduction by
PASCAL BRUCKNER

PENGUIN BOOKS

PENGUIN BOOKS

Published by the Penguin Group
Penguin Group (USA) Inc., 375 Hudson Street, New York, New York 10014, U.S.A.
Penguin Group (Canada), 90 Eglinton Avenue East, Suite 700, Toronto, Ontario, Canada M4P 2Y3
(a division of Pearson Penguin Canada Inc.)
Penguin Books Ltd, 80 Strand, London WC2R 0RL, England
Penguin Ireland, 25 St Stephen's Green, Dublin 2, Ireland (a division of Penguin Books Ltd)
Penguin Group (Australia), 250 Camberwell Road, Camberwell, Victoria 3124, Australia
(a division of Pearson Australia Group Pty Ltd)
Penguin Books India Pvt Ltd, 11 Community Centre, Panchsheel Park, New Delhi – 110 017, India
Penguin Group (NZ), cnr Airborne and Rosedale Roads, Albany, Auckland 1310, New Zealand
(a division of Pearson New Zealand Ltd)
Penguin Books (South Africa) (Pty) Ltd, 24 Sturdee Avenue, Rosebank, Johannesburg 2196, South Africa

Penguin Books Ltd, Registered Offices:
80 Strand, London WC2R 0RL, England

First published in the United States of America by Sun Press 1982
Published in Penguin Books 1988
This edition with an essay by Pascal Bruckner published 2007

10

Copyright © Paul Auster, 1982
All rights reserved

"Paul Auster, or The Heir Intestate" by Pascal Bruckner was published as the afterword to *L'Invention de
la Solitude*, Actes Sud, Paris. Copyright © 1992 by Actes Sud. The English translation by Karen Palmunen
appeared in *Beyond the Red Notebook: Essays on Paul Auster*, edited by Dennis Barone, University of
Pennsylvania Press, 1995. Used by permission of Actes Sud and the University of Pennsylvania Press.

The translations of poems by Stephane Mallarme originally appeared in *The Paris Review* 78.

LIBRARY OF CONGRESS CATALOGING IN PUBLICATION DATA
Auster, Paul, 1947–
The invention of solitude / Paul Auster ; introduction by Pascal Bruckner.
p. cm.
Includes bibliographical references.
Contents: Portrait of an invisible man—The book of memory.
ISBN 978-0-14-311222-8
1. Auster, Paul, 1947–   2. Authors, American—20th century—Biography.   3. Fathers and sons—
United States.   I. Title.
PS3551.U77I5 2007
813'.54—dc22   2006051504

Printed in the United States of America
Set in Adobe Sabon

Contents

Introduction

Paul Auster, or The Heir Intestate

The Invention of Solitude is both the *ars poetica* and the seminal work of Paul Auster. To understand him we must start here; all his books lead us back to this one. Novel-manifesto in two parts, "Portrait of an Invisible Man" and "The Book of Memory," this work immediately sounds the theme of remorse.

Paul Auster was able to become a writer because his father left him a small inheritance that spared him a life of poverty. The father's death not only liberated his son's writing but literally saved his life. The son would never stop repaying this debt, would never finish reimbursing the deceased, in prose, for his fearsome gift. As payment Auster seeks to revive the image of this man he barely knew. The elder Auster, landlord by profession, was an absent character, "a block of impenetrable space in the form of a man" (7), an invisible being, "tourist of his own life" (9). One had the feeling that he never could be located, and he masked this evanescence with perpetual chatter. How could you be yourself in a world where your father was disengaged? This father remained a stranger to Auster, and made Auster a stranger to himself. His father had denied him the usual outlet of youth: rebellion, because one can't rebel against a phantom. And the author, who had to lose his father in order to find him, would respond by filling his novels with figures of weak, colorless, pitiful parents, overwhelmed by their offspring and incapable of assuming fatherhood. Like Pinocchio snatching Geppetto from the jaws of the shark, Paul Auster would save his father from oblivion and, by giving him new life, justify his own existence.

As the story unfolds, sketching an increasingly more complex image of the deceased, one truth becomes evident: reaching one's father requires work. By giving birth to his own parent through words, the author repairs a broken communication and makes it possible for himself, in turn, to become a father. In short, a subtle dialectic directs this plot. According to Auster, proximity is deceptive, and anonymity is not only the misfortune of the masses, or of the cities, but also a cancer gnawing away at the family and marital unit. Human contact often masks a gulf that only death or distance can bridge. We are separated from others by those very things that also connect us; we are separated from ourselves by the illusion of self-knowledge. Just as we must forget ourselves in order to reach a certain level of self-truth, we must also leave others in order to find them in the prism of memory or separation. That which is closest is often the most enigmatic, and distance, like mourning and wandering, is also an instrument of redemption.

In the beginning, therefore, are sin and dispossession. Only an accident, a rupture, will shake the self from its apathy, from the pseudo-intimacy it maintains with itself. It is here that Auster's series of staggering paradoxes begins.

For Auster, confinement is a form of exile. *The Invention of Solitude* can be read as a celebration of rooms and closed spaces. This enclosure has nothing to do with the so-called panegyric of private life, or "cocooning." There is neither public nor private in this novelistic universe since the individual does not own himself. His center is located outside himself. This penchant for narrow spaces, where the spirit can project itself against the walls (the examination of this theme in Hölderlin, Anne Frank, Collodi, Van Gogh, or Vermeer is fascinating) makes the room a kind of mental uterus, site of a second birth. In this enclosure the subject gives birth, in essence, to himself. From mere biological existence he now attains spiritual life. This confinement transforms him into a voluntary castaway, a Robinson Crusoe run aground in the middle of the city, wedged into a tiny fissure of the urban habitat. This shipwreck is necessary, even if it resembles a deferred suicide. The self must die, Auster seems to say, in order to live; there is a redemptive sense to annulment; hence Auster's heroes push themselves to the limit of hunger and physical deprivation. This self-destructive passion, which barely avoids total annihilation (in a way similar to that analyzed by Auster in Knut Hamsun's *Hunger*), transforms this confinement in one's room into a sort of secular asceticism without transcendence, without God. As if the fathers' actual death required the fictitious death of their sons, Auster's character is always ready to offer himself in sacrifice. The only valid existence is that which has experienced extinction.

Auster's work explores a second paradox: death is the first step toward resurrection. Since this life given us by another is invalid, descent into hell is the only way to reclaim an authentic existence, to kill the old man within. Our room is a prison that opens the gates of freedom; the self is a dungeon we must voluntarily enter in order to find escape. If confinement leads to nomadism, the latter in turn will guide the protagonists toward self-reconciliation.

Auster also examines a third paradox: wandering is intimacy's helpmate. In his work, it is fate, ironic and mischievous providence, that breaks down the false barrier between the near and the far, between mine and yours, ours and theirs. No matter how far he roams, the individual will ultimately meet himself; he is inclined to be at home everywhere, since he is not at home in his own house:

During the war, M.'s father had hidden out from the Nazis for several months in a Paris *chambre de bonne*. Eventually, he managed to escape, made his way to America, and began a new life. Years passed, more than twenty years. M. had been born, had grown up, and now was going off to study in Paris. Once there he spent several difficult weeks looking for a place to live. Just when he was about to give up in despair, he found a small *chambre de bonne*. Immediately upon moving in, he wrote a letter to his father to tell him the good news. A week or so later he received a reply: your address, wrote M.'s father, that is the same building I hid out in during the war. He then went on to describe the details of the room. It turned out to be the same room his son had rented. (80)

All of Auster is there in this love of coincidences that rhyme the most remote, improbable events. He excels at sprinkling his characters' adventures with correlations, which have no a priori meaning, but to which the story gives unexpected consequences. Noting the signs that fate strews along our path is the only way to combat the arbitrary: suddenly, in the randomness of existence, a certain order appears just below the surface, an order which seems mysteriously to control us. There is meaning in the world, but this meaning is only suggested, never clearly expressed. Therefore, everything in Paul Auster's work occurs by chance; and what better image of chance than an inheritance—an event as harmful as it is beneficial. It is as if money of the deceased were an oppressive gift that could drag us, with its donor, beyond the grave. The novelist's challenge here is to endow this image of the unexpected with the weight of necessity, to continue converting the improbable into the inevitable, to avoid gratuitousness. The novelist must also be a bit of an acrobat: plunging his characters into confusing situations, then weaving among them a fabric of dense analogies, linking the episodes together in such an inevitable manner that the reader cannot imagine the story occurring any other way. This penchant for reversals, for sudden about-faces, also places Paul Auster in the picaresque tradition, at the opposite extreme from his avowed masters, Kafka and Beckett.

Wandering, in Auster, has this original aspect: rather than pitting the individual against a cold, hostile world, it forces him to confront himself and the scattered fragments of his existence. Everything relates back to the self, and, while the closed room serves as a microcosm, the outer world itself becomes an enclosure, which speaks in veiled tones. "Home" is everywhere since the self is not at home with itself. *The Invention of Solitude* announces a theme that Paul Auster will raise to the level of a true obsession: nomadism as a means of cloistering oneself; introspection as a means of escape. (Hence the appeal of pseudonyms and non-places in *City of Glass*, the characters' capacity to take on other identities, the kaleidoscope of doubles, of contingent selves, the suspended moments when a person almost chooses to become someone else, illusions that bathe this

trilogy in a kind of subdued Platonism.) "Exiling himself in order to find out where he was" (16). This formula that Auster applies to Thoreau suits Auster perfectly. He is able to reverse the
language of mobility and immobility, of the wanderer and the
sedentary. Through escape, we experience intimacy; through
confrontation, estrangement. And this reversal may be rooted in
the experience of a young boy who, in the presence of his father,
felt total absence and solitude.

It is easy to see what distinguishes Paul Auster from other
contemporary writers and to see why he is so successful. There
is no one less narcissistic than this novelist obsessed with the
self. This is because he challenges two attitudes that are common today: the proud, in-control self with no ties and no past,
and the traditionalist or minority, proud of his identity, his
roots, his people. Auster's point of view is different: he recog-
nizes his connection to a family, a tradition, a culture, but he
also realizes that this is a highly problematic link. In short, to
paraphrase the famous verse of René Char, the legacy is ambigu-
ous: the will is missing. Since nothing has a priori meaning—
this, the very curse of modernity—the self, like solitude and
tradition, must literally be invented and re-created. Auster is
not an advocate of difference; he claims no particular status,
does not ghettoize himself in any group. He does not seek what
separates people, but, rather, what brings them together; and
what they have in common is a similar confusion about their
identity. But he has also avoided what has been killing Western
literature for the past twenty years: the invasive proliferation
of autobiography, of the diary, of self-preoccupation as a genre
in and of itself. This literature, which tends to narrow rather
than broaden experience, is most frequently reduced to a bitter
whine, since it conveys above all the impossibility of escaping
the self. And it is the unfortunate irony of these books, devoted
to revealing the individual's most intimate essence, their sub-
jectivity unparalleled, that they all end up resembling each
other, as if written by the same person. With these publications
writing becomes an isolating activity, which contradicts its intended universality. And its fanatical celebration of the writer's
uniqueness or interiority repels the reader, who is reluctant

to let himself be trapped or fascinated. Instead of creating a world where all might live together, the writer takes from the community its common tool, language, which he then uses to distance himself from the group and to express his own uniqueness. All these voices raised in soliloquy, detailing their petty problems, create a universe of mutual deafness where each person, talking about himself, no longer has the time to listen to others.

Unlike this orgy of egotism, Auster's *The Invention of Solitude* is a story whose strength lies in its very simplicity. Through this apparent banality the reader finds himself, and narrative regains its true identity. It is once again a homeland open to all without distinction, a place of welcome: "I don't feel that I was telling the story of my life so much as using myself to explore certain questions that are common to us all," Auster says in an interview. Auster's hero is not someone who prefers himself, to repeat Brecht's definition of the bourgeois, but someone who doubts and communicates this doubt to the reader. Readers identify less with the protagonists' adventures than with the strangeness they feel about themselves—for whom being or becoming someone constitutes the ultimate difficulty. Auster does not condemn, like classical writers, the self's wretchedness in the face of God's grandeur. He does worse: he dissolves this self, declares it a nonentity. Uncertainty eats into the core of our being; our heart is empty or cluttered with so much static that it seems to hold nothing.

This work clearly also expresses the genealogical passion of the uprooted, and it is not insignificant that Auster is an American entirely oriented toward Europe. But this proximity is misleading. A reading of Auster produces a double sensation of familiarity and disorientation, for Auster, deeply anchored in the New World, does not write European books in America; he enriches the American novel with European themes. *The Invention of Solitude,* a tribute to Auster's departed father, continues in the second part with a warm greeting to all those poets and thinkers who have influenced the author. Through writing we can choose other fathers to compensate for our own, discover a spiritual link, go beyond ourselves. Memory is immersion in the past of all those others who comprise us. The narrator distinguishes, one by one, these voices that speak through him that must be quieted before his true inner voice can be heard. But this goal is impossible to attain: the palimpsest self, like an ever-unpeeling onion, resists categorization. This peregrination through the continents of memory may be a marvelous journey, but it does not succeed in easing the pain. No matter how far it roams, the self is always haunted and tortured by the others; it is a room full of strangers and intruders who speak in his place. Auster's approach is not, of course, the same as Proust's anamnesis, an attempt to compensate for life's imperfections by fixing the flight of time in a work of art. It is an eternal quest, without guaranteed results, which can never achieve closure. A detective of the self, Paul Auster applies an uncompromising narrative skill to a metaphysical quest: Why is there a self rather than nothing? To facilitate this task, he presents his fiction in the protective guise of the detective novel. In the end, however, nothing is resolved. Each book is a collective work, the tribute of a writer to all those, past and present, who have helped him create. But this courtesy toward the dead, calling them to his bedside, inviting them to a vast, cross-century symposium, does not expunge the debt. Just as a son can never stop paying for the death of the father who gave him life, so, too, the self can never stop paying its due. It could even define itself this way: the eternal debtor always under obligation to others. That is why this literature must tirelessly rewrite its missing testament. And if, as the famous saying goes, a prophet is someone who remembers the future, the writer, according to Auster, is someone who predicts the past in order first to capture and then to free himself from it. But memory's archives are both chaotic and infinite, and the clerk who attempts to record them will soon get lost in the maze.

Paul Auster completely renews the coming-of-age novel. With unusual talent he reveals how painful it is to be an individual today thrust out from the protective shell of a belief or tradition. After these extensive investigations he offers no final wisdom. Each of his novels outlines the beginning of a redemption, which it subsequently rejects. The lack of response, or of comfort, the stubborn refusal to abandon the pain of this issue, that is the strength of these works. As each plot is unraveled an increasingly more obscure enigma is revealed. His literature is like a brief burst of sunshine between a hidden and an exposed mystery, a glimmer between two shades of darkness. "Just because you wander in the desert, it does not mean there is a promised land." All his characters—vagabonds, gamblers, semi-tramps, magnificent losers, failed writers—are under way. Like Marco Stanley Fogg at the end of *Moon Palace,* facing the ocean in the hazy moonlight, these characters are more serene at the end of the day, but they are never sovereign. Their chaotic odyssey never ends in peace, and they always fail to regain their lost innocence. Writing never removes the agony, but, rather, alters and deepens it. Writing is futility because it fails to express the experience of loss and renunciation. Perhaps Paul Auster's rich works already prefigure what certain historians foresee as the religion of the future: Christian-Buddhism, that is, a concern with personal salvation linked to an acute awareness of uncertainty and the void.

—PASCAL BRUCKNER
(*Translated by Karen Palmunen*)

THE INVENTION
of SOLITUDE

PORTRAIT OF AN INVISIBLE MAN

In searching out the truth be ready for the unexpected, for it is difficult to find and puzzling when you find it.

—Heraclitus

One day there is life. A man, for example, in the best of health, not even old, with no history of illness. Everything is as it was, as it will always be. He goes from one day to the next, minding his own business, dreaming only of the life that lies before him. And then, suddenly, it happens there is death. A man lets out a little sigh, he slumps down in his chair, and it is death. The suddenness of it leaves no room for thought, gives the mind no chance to seek out a word that might comfort it. We are left with nothing but death, the irreducible fact of our own mortality. Death after a long illness we can accept with resignation. Even accidental death we can ascribe to fate. But for a man to die of no apparent cause, for a man to die simply because he is a man, brings us so close to the invisible boundary between life and death that we no longer know which side we are on. Life becomes death, and it is as if this death has owned this life all along. Death without warning. Which is to say: life stops. And it can stop at any moment.

The news of my father's death came to me three weeks ago. It was Sunday morning, and I was in the kitchen preparing breakfast for my small son, Daniel. Upstairs my wife was still in bed, warm under the quilts, luxuriating in a few extra hours of sleep. Winter in the country: a world of silence, wood smoke, whiteness. My mind was filled with thoughts about the piece I had been writing the night before, and I was looking ahead to the afternoon when I would be able to get back to work. Then the phone rang. I knew instantly that there was trouble. No one calls at eight o'clock on a Sunday morning unless it is to give

news that cannot wait. And news that cannot wait is always bad
news.

I could not muster a single ennobling thought.

Even before we packed our bags and set out on the three-hour
drive to New Jersey, I knew that I would have to write about
my father. I had no plan, had no precise idea of what this
meant. I cannot even remember making a decision about it. It
was simply there, a certainty, an obligation that began to im-
pose itself on me the moment I was given the news. I thought:
my father is gone. If I do not act quickly, his entire life will vanish along with him.

Looking back on it now, even from so short a distance as
three weeks, I find this a rather curious reaction. I had always
imagined that death would numb me, immobilize me with grief.
But now that it had happened, I did not shed any tears, I did not
feel as though the world had collapsed around me. In some
strange way, I was remarkably prepared to accept this death, in
spite of its suddenness. What disturbed me was something else,
something unrelated to death or my response to it: the realiza-
tion that my father had left no traces.

He had no wife, no family that depended on him, no one
whose life would be altered by his absence. A brief moment of
shock, perhaps, on the part of scattered friends, sobered as
much by the thought of capricious death as by the loss of their
friend, followed by a short period of mourning, and then nothing. Eventually, it would be as though he had never lived at all.

Even before his death he had been absent, and long ago the
people closest to him had learned to accept this absence, to treat
it as the fundamental quality of his being. Now that he was
gone, it would not be difficult for the world to absorb the fact
that he was gone forever. The nature of his life had prepared the
world for his death—had been a kind of death by anticipation—
and if and when he was remembered, it would be dimly, no
more than dimly.

Devoid of passion, either for a thing, a person, or an idea, incapable or unwilling to reveal himself under any circumstances,
he had managed to keep himself at a distance from life, to avoid

immersion in the quick of things. He ate, he went to work, he had friends, he played tennis, and yet for all that he was not there. In the deepest, most unalterable sense, he was an invisible man. Invisible to others, and most likely invisible to himself as well. If, while he was alive, I kept looking for him, kept trying to find the father who was not there, now that he is dead I still feel as though I must go on looking for him. Death has not changed anything. The only difference is that I have run out of time.

For fifteen years he had lived alone. Doggedly, opaquely, as if immune to the world. He did not seem to be a man occupying space, but rather a block of impenetrable space in the form of a man. The world bounced off him, shattered against him, at times adhered to him—but it never got through. For fifteen years he haunted an enormous house, all by himself, and it was in that house that he died.

For a short while we had lived there as a family—my father, my mother, my sister, and I. After my parents were divorced, everyone dispersed: my mother began a new life, I went off to college, and my sister stayed with my mother until she, too, went off to school. Only my father remained. Because of a clause in the divorce agreement which stipulated that my mother still owned a share of the house and would be given half the proceeds whenever it was sold (which made my father reluctant to sell), or from some secret refusal to change his life (so as not to show the world that the divorce had affected him in a way he could not control), or simply from inertia, an emotional lethargy that prevented him from taking any action, he stayed on, living alone in a house that could have accommodated six or seven people.

It was an impressive place: old, solidly built, in the Tudor style, with leaded windows, a slate roof, and rooms of royal proportions. Buying it had been a big step for my parents, a sign of growing wealth. This was the best neighborhood in town, and although it was not a pleasant place to live (especially for children), its prestige outweighed its deadliness. Given the fact that he wound up spending the rest of his life in that house, it is ironic that my father at first resisted moving there. He complained about the price (a constant theme), and when at last he relented, it was with grudging bad humor. Even so, he paid in cash. All in one go. No mortgage, no monthly payments. It was 1959, and business was going well for him.

Always a man of habit, he would leave for work early in the morning, work hard all day, and then, when he came home (on those days he did not work late), take a short nap before dinner. Sometime during our first week in the new house, before we had properly moved in, he made a curious kind of mistake. Instead of driving home to the new house after work, he went directly to the old one, as he had done for years, parked his car in the driveway, walked into the house through the back door, climbed the stairs, entered the bedroom, lay down on the bed, and went to sleep. He slept for about an hour. Needless to say, when the new mistress of the house returned to find a strange man sleeping in her bed, she was a little surprised. But unlike Goldilocks, my father did not jump up and run away. The confusion was eventually settled, and everyone had a good laugh. Even today, it still makes me laugh. And yet, for all that, I cannot help regarding it as a pathetic story. It is one thing for a man to drive to his old house by mistake, but it is quite another, I think, for him not to notice that anything has changed inside it. Even the most tired or distracted mind has a corner of pure, animal response, and can give the body a sense of where it is. One would have to be nearly unconscious not to see, or at least not to feel, that the house was no longer the same. "Habit," as one of Beckett's characters says, "is a great deadener." And if the mind is unable to respond to the physical evidence, what will it do when confronted with the emotional evidence?

During those last fifteen years he changed almost nothing in the house. He did not add any furniture, he did not remove any furniture. The walls remained the same color, the pots and pans were not replaced, even my mother's dresses were not thrown out—but stored away in an attic closet. The very size of the house absolved him from having to make any decisions about the things it contained. It was not that he was clinging to the past, trying to preserve the house as a museum. On the contrary, he seemed to be unaware of what he was doing. It was negligence that governed him, not memory, and even though he went on living in that house all those years, he lived in it as a stranger might have. As the years went by, he spent less and less time there. He ate nearly all his meals in restaurants, arranged his social calendar so as to be busy every night, and used the house as little more than a place to sleep. Once, several years ago, I happened to mention to him how much money I had earned from my writing and translating during the previous year (a pittance by any standard, but more than I had ever made before), and his amused response was that he spent more than that just on eating out. The point is: his life was not centered around the place where he lived. His house was just one of many stopping places in a restless, unmoored existence, and this lack of center had the effect of turning him into a perpetual outsider, a tourist of his own life. You never had the feeling that he could be located.

Still, the house seems important to me, if only to the extent that it was neglected—symptomatic of a state of mind that, otherwise inaccessible, manifested itself in the concrete images of unconscious behavior. The house became the metaphor of my father's life, the exact and faithful representation of his inner world. For although he kept the house tidy and preserved it more or less as it had been, it underwent a gradual and ineluctable process of disintegration. He was neat, he always put things back in their proper place, but nothing was cared for, nothing was ever cleaned. The furniture, especially in the rooms he rarely visited, was covered with dust, cobwebs, the signs of total neglect; the kitchen stove was so encrusted with charred food that it had become unsalvageable; in the cupboard, sometimes languishing on the shelves for years: bug-infested packages of flour, stale crackers, bags of sugar that had turned into solid blocks, bottles of syrup that could no longer be opened. Whenever he prepared a meal for himself, he would immediately and assiduously do the dishes—but rinse them only, never using soap, so that every cup, every saucer, every plate was coated with a film of dingy grease. Throughout the house: the

window shades, which were kept drawn at all times, had become so threadbare that the slightest tug would pull them apart.
Leaks sprang and stained the furniture, the furnace never gave
off enough heat, the shower did not work. The house became
shabby, depressing to walk into. You felt as if you were entering
the house of a blind man.

His friends and family, sensing the madness of the way he
lived in that house, kept urging him to sell it and move somewhere else. But he always managed to ward them off with a
non-committal "I'm happy here," or "The house suits me fine."
In the end, however, he did decide to move. At the very end. In
the last phone conversation we ever had, ten days before he
died, he told me the house had been sold and that the closing
was set for February first, about three weeks away. He wanted
to know if there was anything in the house I could use, and I
agreed to come down for a visit with my wife and Daniel on the
first free day that opened up. He died before we had a chance to
make it.

There is nothing more terrible, I learned, than having to face
the objects of a dead man. Things are inert: they have meaning
only in function of the life that makes use of them. When that
life ends, the things change, even though they remain the same.
They are there and yet not there: tangible ghosts, condemned
to survive in a world they no longer belong to. What is one to
think, for example, of a closetful of clothes waiting silently
to be worn again by a man who will not be coming back to
open the door? Or the stray packets of condoms strewn among
brimming drawers of underwear and socks? Or an electric razor sitting in the bathroom, still clogged with the whisker dust
of the last shave? Or a dozen empty tubes of hair coloring hidden away in a leather traveling case?—suddenly revealing
things one has no desire to see, no desire to know. There is a
poignancy to it, and also a kind of horror. In themselves, the
things mean nothing, like the cooking utensils of some vanished civilization. And yet they say something to us, standing
there not as objects but as remnants of thought, of consciousness, emblems of the solitude in which a man comes to make

decisions about himself: whether to color his hair, whether to wear this or that shirt, whether to live, whether to die. And the futility of it all once there is death.

Each time I opened a drawer or poked my head into a closet, I felt like an intruder, a burglar ransacking the secret places of a man's mind. I kept expecting my father to walk in, to stare at me in disbelief, and ask me what the hell I thought I was doing. It didn't seem fair that he couldn't protest. I had no right to invade his privacy.

A hastily scrawled telephone number on the back of a business card that read: H. Limeburg—Garbage Cans of All Descriptions. Photographs of my parents' honeymoon in Niagara Falls, 1946: my mother sitting nervously on top of a bull for one of those funny shots that are never funny, and a sudden sense of how unreal the world has always been, even in its prehistory. A drawer full of hammers, nails, and more than twenty screwdrivers. A filing cabinet stuffed with canceled checks from 1953 and the cards I received for my sixth birthday. And then, buried at the bottom of a drawer in the bathroom: the monogrammed toothbrush that had once belonged to my mother and which had not been touched or looked at for more than fifteen years.

The list is inexhaustible.

It soon became apparent to me that my father had done almost nothing to prepare himself for his departure. The only signs of the impending move I could detect in the whole house were a few cartons of books—trivial books (out of date atlases, a fifty-year-old introduction to electronics, a high school Latin grammar, ancient law books) that he had been planning to give away to charity. Other than that, nothing. No empty boxes waiting to be filled. No pieces of furniture given away or sold. No arrangements made with a moving company. It was as though he had not been able to face it. Rather than empty the house, he had simply willed himself to die. Death was a way out, the only legitimate escape.

There was no escape for me, however. The thing had to be done, and there was no one else to do it. For ten days I went through his things, cleared out the house, got it ready for the new owners. It was a miserable time, but also an oddly humorous time, a time of reckless and absurd decisions: sell it, throw it out, give it away. My wife and I bought a big wooden slide for eighteen-month old Daniel and set it up in the living room. He thrived on the chaos: rummaging among the things, putting lampshades on his head, flinging plastic poker chips around the house, running through the vast spaces of the gradually emptying rooms. At night my wife and I would lie under monolithic quilts watching trashy movies on television. Until the television, too, was given away. There was trouble with the furnace, and if I forgot to fill it with water, it would shut off. One morning we woke up to find that the temperature in the house had dropped to forty degrees. Twenty times a day the phone rang, and twenty times a day I told someone that my father was dead. I had become a furniture salesman, a moving man, a messenger of bad tidings.

The house began to resemble the set for a trite comedy of manners. Relatives swooped in, asking for this piece of furniture or that piece of dinnerware, trying on my father's suits, overturning boxes, chattering away like geese. Auctioneers came to examine the merchandise ("Nothing upholstered, it's not worth a nickel"), turned up their noses, and walked out. Garbage men clumped in with heavy boots and hauled off mountains of trash. The water man read the water meter, the gas man read the gas meter, the oil men read the oil gauge. (One of them, I forget which, who had been given a lot of trouble by my father over the years, said to me with savage complicity, "I don't like to say this"—meaning he did—"but your father was an obnoxious bastard.") The real estate agent came to buy some furniture for the new owners and wound up taking a mirror for herself. A woman who ran a curio shop bought my mother's old hats. A junkman came with a team of assistants (four black men named Luther, Ulysses, Tommy Pride, and Joe Sapp) and carted away everything from a set of barbels to a broken toaster. By the time it was over, nothing was left. Not even a postcard. Not even a thought.

If there was a single worst moment for me during those days, it came when I walked across the front lawn in the pouring rain to dump an armful of my father's ties into the back of a Good Will Mission truck. There must have been more than a hundred ties, and many of them I remembered from my childhood: the patterns, the colors, the shapes that had been embedded in my earliest consciousness, as clearly as my father's face had been. To see myself throwing them away like so much junk was intolerable to me, and it was then, at the precise instant I tossed them into the truck, that I came closest to tears. More than seeing the coffin itself being lowered into the ground, the act of throwing away these ties seemed to embody for me the idea of burial. I finally understood that my father was dead.

Yesterday one of the neighborhood children came here to play with Daniel. A girl of about three and a half who has recently learned that big people were once children, too, and that even her own mother and father have parents. At one point she picked up the telephone and launched into a pretend conversation, then turned to me and said, "Paul, it's your father. He wants to talk to you." It was gruesome. I thought: there's a ghost at the other end of the line, and he really does want to talk to me. It was a few moments before I could speak. "No," I finally blurted out. "It can't be my father. He wouldn't be calling today. He's somewhere else."

I waited until she had hung up the phone and then walked out of the room.

In his bedroom closet I had found several hundred photographs—stashed away in faded manila envelopes, affixed to the black pages of warped albums, scattered loosely in drawers. From the way they had been stored I gathered he never looked at them, had even forgotten they were there. One very big album, bound in expensive leather with a gold-stamped title on the cover—This is Our Life: The Austers—was totally blank inside. Someone, probably my mother, had once gone to the trouble of ordering this album, but no one had ever bothered to fill it.

Back home, I pored over these pictures with a fascination bordering on mania. I found them irresistible, precious, the equivalent of holy relics. It seemed that they could tell me things I had never known before, reveal some previously hidden truth, and I studied each one intensely, absorbing the least detail, the most insignificant shadow, until all the images had become a part of me. I wanted nothing to be lost.

Death takes a man's body away from him. In life, a man and his body are synonymous; in death, there is the man and there is his body. We say, "This is the body of X," as if this body, which had once been the man himself, not something that represented him or belonged to him, but the very man called X, were suddenly of no importance. When a man walks into a room and you shake hands with him, you do not feel that you are shaking hands with his hand, or shaking hands with his body, you are shaking hands with *him*. Death changes that. This is the body of X, not this is X. The syntax is entirely different. Now we are talking about two things instead of one, implying that the man continues to exist, but only as an idea, a cluster of images and memories in the minds of other people. As for the body, it is no more than flesh and bones, a heap of pure matter.

Discovering these photographs was important to me because they seemed to reaffirm my father's physical presence in the world, to give me the illusion that he was still there. The fact that many of these pictures were ones I had never seen before, especially the ones of his youth, gave me the odd sensation that I was meeting him for the first time, that a part of him was only just beginning to exist. I had lost my father. But at the same time, I had also found him. As long as I kept these pictures before my eyes, as long as I continued to study them with my complete attention, it was as though he were still alive, even in death. Or if not alive, at least not dead. Or rather, somehow suspended, locked in a universe that had nothing to do with death, in which death could never make an entrance.

Most of these pictures did not tell me anything new, but they helped to fill in gaps, confirm impressions, offer proof where none had existed before. A series of snapshots of him as a bachelor, for example, probably taken over a number of years, gives a precise account of certain aspects of his personality that had been submerged during the years of his marriage, a side of him I did not begin to see until after his divorce: my father as prankster, as man about town, as good time Charlie. In picture after picture he is standing with women, usually two or three, all of them affecting comical poses, their arms perhaps around each other, or two of them sitting on his lap, or else a theatrical kiss for the benefit of no one but the person taking the picture. In the background: a mountain, a tennis court, perhaps a swimming pool or a log cabin. These were the pictures brought back from weekend jaunts to various Catskill resorts in the company of his bachelor friends: play tennis, have a good time with the girls. He carried on in this way until he was thirty-four.

It was a life that suited him, and I can see why he went back to it after his marriage broke up. For a man who finds life tolerable only by staying on the surface of himself, it is natural to be satisfied with offering no more than this surface to others. There are few demands to be met, and no commitment is required. Marriage, on the other hand, closes the door. Your existence is confined to a narrow space in which you are constantly forced to reveal yourself—and therefore, constantly obliged to look into yourself, to examine your own depths. When the door is open there is never any problem: you can always escape. You can avoid unwanted confrontations, either with yourself or with another, simply by walking away.

My father's capacity for evasion was almost limitless. Because the domain of the other was unreal to him, his incursions into that domain were made with a part of himself he considered to be equally unreal, another self he had trained as an actor to represent him in the empty comedy of the world-at-large. This surrogate self was essentially a tease, a hyperactive child, a fabricator of tall tales. It could not take anything seriously.

Because nothing mattered, he gave himself the freedom to do anything he wanted (sneaking into tennis clubs, pretending to be a restaurant critic in order to get a free meal), and the charm he exercised to make his conquests was precisely what made these conquests meaningless. With the vanity of a woman he hid the truth about his age, made up stories about his business dealings, talked about himself only obliquely—in the third person, as if about an acquaintance of his ("There's a friend of mine who has this problem; what do you think he should do about it? . . ."). Whenever a situation became too tight for him, whenever he felt pushed to the verge of having to reveal himself, he would wriggle out of it by telling a lie. Eventually, the lie came automatically and was indulged in for its own sake. The principle was to say as little as possible. If people never learned the truth about him, then they couldn't turn around and use it against him later. The lie was a way of buying protection. What people saw when he appeared before them, then, was not really him, but a person he had invented, an artificial creature he could manipulate in order to manipulate others. He himself remained invisible, a puppeteer working the strings of his alterego from a dark, solitary place behind the curtain.

For the last ten or twelve years of his life he had one steady lady friend, and this was the woman who went out with him in public, who played the role of official companion. Every now and then there was some vague talk of marriage (at her insistence), and everyone assumed that this was the only woman he had anything to do with. After his death, however, other women began to step forward. This one had loved him, that one had worshipped him, another one was going to marry him. The principal girlfriend was shocked to learn about these other women: my father had never breathed a word about them to her. Each one had been fed a different line, and each one thought she had possessed him entirely. As it turned out, none of them knew the slightest thing about him. He had managed to elude them all.

Solitary. But not in the sense of being alone. Not solitary in the way Thoreau was, for example, exiling himself in order to find out where he was; not solitary in the way Jonah was, praying for deliverance in the belly of the whale. Solitary in the sense of retreat. In the sense of not having to see himself, of not having to see himself being seen by anyone else.

Talking to him was a trying experience. Either he would be

absent, as he usually was, or he would assault you with a brittle jocularity, which was merely another form of absence. It was like trying to make yourself understood by a senile old man. You talked, and there would be no response, or a response that was inappropriate, showing that he hadn't been following the drift of your words. In recent years, whenever I spoke to him on the phone I would find myself saying more than I normally do, becoming aggressively talkative, chatting away in a futile attempt to hold his attention, to provoke a response. Afterwards, I would invariably feel foolish for having tried so hard.

He did not smoke, he did not drink. No hunger for sensual pleasures, no thirst for intellectual pleasures. Books bored him, and it was the rare movie or play that did not put him to sleep. Even at parties you would see him struggling to keep his eyes open, and more often than not he would succumb, falling asleep in a chair as the conversations swirled around him. A man without appetites. You felt that nothing could ever intrude on him, that he had no need of anything the world had to offer.

At thirty-four, marriage. At fifty-two, divorce. In one sense, it lasted years, but in fact it did not last more than a few days. He was never a married man, never a divorced man, but a life-long bachelor who happened to have had an interlude of marriage. Although he did not shirk his outward duties as a husband (he was faithful, he provided for his wife and children, he shouldered all his responsibilities), it was clear that he was not cut out to play this role. He simply had no talent for it.

My mother was just twenty-one when she married him. His conduct during the brief courtship had been chaste. No daring overtures, none of the aroused male's breathless assaults. Now and then they would hold hands, exchange a polite good-night kiss. Love, in so many words, was never declared by either one of them. By the time the wedding came, they were little more than strangers.

It was not long before my mother realized her mistake. Even before the honeymoon was over (that honeymoon, so fully documented in the photographs I found: the two of them sitting together, for instance, on a rock at the edge of a perfectly still lake, a broad path of sunlight behind them leading to the pine slope in shadow, my father with his arms around my mother, and the two of them looking at each other, smiling timidly, as if the photographer had made them hold the pose an instant too long), even before the honeymoon was over, my mother knew the marriage would not work. She went to her mother in tears and said she wanted to leave him. Somehow, her mother managed to persuade her to go back and give it a chance. And then, before the dust had settled, she found herself pregnant. And suddenly it was too late to do anything.

I think of it sometimes: how I was conceived in that Niagara Falls resort for honeymooners. Not that it matters where it happened. But the thought of what must have been a passionless embrace, a blind, dutiful groping between chilly hotel sheets, has never failed to humble me into an awareness of my own contingency. Niagara Falls. Or the hazard of two bodies joining. And then me, a random homunculus, like some dare-devil in a barrel, shooting over the falls.

A little more than eight months later, on the morning of her twenty-second birthday, my mother woke up and told my father that the baby was coming. Ridiculous, he said, that baby's not due for another three weeks—and promptly went off to work, leaving her without a car.

She waited. Thought maybe he was right. Waited a little more, then called a sister-in-law and asked to be driven to the hospital. My aunt stayed with my mother throughout the day, calling my father every few hours to ask him to come. Later, he would say, I'm busy now, I'll get there when I can.

At a little past midnight I poked my way into the world, ass first, no doubt screaming.

My mother waited for my father to show up, but he did not arrive until the next morning—accompanied by his mother, who wanted to inspect grandchild number seven. A short, nervous visit, and then off again to work.

She cried, of course. After all, she was young, and she had not expected it to mean so little to him. But he could never understand such things. Not in the beginning, and not in the end.

It was never possible for him to be where he was. For as long as he lived, he was somewhere else, between here and there. But never really here. And never really there.

Thirty years later, this same little drama was repeated. This time I was there, and I saw it with my own eyes.

After my own son was born I had thought: surely this will please him. Isn't every man pleased to become a grandfather?

I had wanted to see him doting on the baby, for him to offer me proof that he was, after all, capable of demonstrating some feeling—that he did, after all, have feelings in the way other people did. And if he could show affection for his grandson, then wouldn't it be an indirect way of showing affection for me? You do not stop hungering for your father's love, even after you are grown up.

But then, people do not change. All told, my father saw his grandson only three or four times, and at no time was he able to distinguish him from the impersonal mass of babies born into the world every day. Daniel was just two weeks old when he first laid eyes on him. I can remember the day vividly: a blistering Sunday at the end of June, heat-wave weather, the country air gray with moisture. My father pulled up in his car, saw my wife putting the baby into the carriage for a nap, and walked over to say hello. He poked his head into the carriage for a tenth of a second, straightened up and said to her, "A beautiful baby. Good luck with it," and then proceeded to walk on into the house. He might just as well have been talking about some stranger's baby encountered in line at the supermarket. For the rest of his visit that day he did not look at Daniel, and not once, ever, did he ask to hold him.

All this, merely as an example.

Impossible, I realize, to enter another's solitude. If it is true that we can ever come to know another human being, even to a small degree, it is only to the extent that he is willing to make himself known. A man will say: I am cold. Or else he will say nothing, and we will see him shivering. Either way, we will know that he is cold. But what of the man who says nothing and does not shiver? Where all is intractable, where all is hermetic and evasive, one can do no more than observe. But whether one can make sense of what he observes is another matter entirely.

I do not want to presume anything.

He never talked about himself, never seemed to know there was anything he *could* talk about. It was as though his inner life eluded even him.

He could not talk about it, and therefore he passed over it in silence.

If there is nothing, then, but silence, is it not presumptuous of me to speak? And yet: if there had been anything more than silence, would I have felt the need to speak in the first place?

My choices are limited. I can remain silent, or else I can speak of things that cannot be verified. At the very least, I want to put down the facts, to offer them as straightforwardly as possible, and let them say whatever they have to say. But even the facts do not always tell the truth.

He was so implacably neutral on the surface, his behavior was so flatly predictable, that everything he did came as a surprise. One could not believe there was such a man—who lacked feeling, who wanted so little of others. And if there was not such a man, that means there was another man, a man hidden inside the man who was not there, and the trick of it, then, is to find him. On the condition that he is there to be found.

To recognize, right from the start, that the essence of this project is failure.

Earliest memory: his absence. For the first years of my life he would leave for work early in the morning, before I was awake, and come home long after I had been put to bed. I was my mother's boy, and I lived in her orbit. I was a little moon circling her gigantic earth, a mote in the sphere of her gravity, and I controlled the tides, the weather, the forces of feeling. His refrain to her was: Don't fuss so much, you'll spoil him. But my health was not good, and she used this to justify the attention she lavished on me. We spent a lot of time together, she in her loneliness and I in my cramps, waiting patiently in doctors' offices for someone to quell the insurrection that continually raged in my stomach. Even then, I would cling to these doctors in a desperate sort of way, wanting them to hold me. From the very beginning, it seems, I was looking for my father, looking frantically for anyone who resembled him.

Later memories: a craving. My mind always ready to deny the facts at the slightest excuse, I mulishly went on hoping for something that was never given to me—or given to me so rarely and arbitrarily that it seemed to happen outside the range of normal experience, in a place where I would never be able to live for more than a few moments at a time. It was not that I felt he disliked me. It was just that he seemed distracted, unable to look in my direction. And more than anything else, I wanted him to take notice of me.

Anything, even the least thing, was enough. How, for example, when the family once went to a crowded restaurant on a Sunday and we had to wait for our table, my father took me outside, produced a tennis ball (from where?), put a penny on the sidewalk, and proceeded to play a game with me: hit the penny with the tennis ball. I could not have been more than eight or nine years old.

In retrospect, nothing could have been more trivial. And yet the fact that I had been included, that my father had casually asked me to share his boredom with him, nearly crushed me with happiness.

More often, there were disappointments. For a moment he would seem to have changed, to have opened up a little, and then, suddenly, he would not be there anymore. The one time I managed to persuade him to take me to a football game (the Giants versus the Chicago Cardinals, at Yankee Stadium or the Polo Grounds, I forget which), he abruptly stood up from his seat in the middle of the fourth quarter and said, "It's time to go now." He wanted to "beat the crowd" and avoid getting stuck in traffic. Nothing I said could convince him to stay, and so we left, just like that, with the game going full tilt. Unearthly despair as I followed him down the concrete ramps, and then, even worse, in the parking lot, with the noise of the invisible crowd roaring behind me.

You could not trust him to know what you wanted, to anticipate what you might have been feeling. The fact that you had to tell him yourself vitiated the pleasure in advance, disrupted a dreamed-of harmony before a note could be played. And then, even if you did tell him, it was not at all sure that he would understand what you meant.

I remember a day very like today. A drizzling Sunday, lethargy and quiet in the house: the world at half-speed. My father was taking a nap, or had just awoken from one, and somehow I was on the bed with him, the two of us alone in the room. Tell me a story. It must have begun like that. And because he was not doing anything, because he was still drowsing in the languor of the afternoon, he did just what I asked, launching into a story without missing a beat. I remember it all so clearly. It seems as if I have just walked out of that room, with its gray light and tangle of quilts on the bed, as if, simply by closing my eyes, I could walk back into it any time I want.

He told me of his prospecting days in South America. It was a tale of high adventure, fraught with mortal dangers, hair-raising escapes, and improbable twists of fortune: hacking his way through the jungle with a machete, fighting off bandits with his bare hands, shooting his donkey when it broke its leg. His language was flowery and convoluted, probably an echo of the books he himself had read as a boy. But it was precisely this literary style that enchanted me. Not only was he telling me new things about himself, unveiling to me the world of his distant past, but he was telling it with new and strange words. This language was just as important as the story itself. It belonged to it, and in some sense was indistinguishable from it. Its very strangeness was proof of authenticity.

It did not occur to me to think this might have been a made-up story. For years afterward I went on believing it. Even when I had passed the point when I should have known better, I still felt there might have been some truth to it. It gave me something to hold on to about my father, and I was reluctant to let go. At last I had an explanation for his mysterious evasions, his indifference to me. He was a romantic figure, a man with a dark and exciting past, and his present life was only a kind of stopping place, a way of biding his time until he took off on his next adventure. He was working out his plan, figuring out how to retrieve the gold that lay buried deep in the heart of the Andes.

In the back of my mind: a desire to do something extraordinary, to impress him with an act of heroic proportions. The more aloof he was, the higher the stakes became for me. But if a boy's will is tenacious and idealistic, it is also absurdly practical. I was only ten years old, and there was no child for me to save from a burning building, no sailors to rescue at sea. On the other hand, I was a good baseball player, the star of my Little League team, and although my father had no interest in baseball, I thought that if he saw me play, just once, he would begin to see me in a new light.

Finally he did come. My mother's parents were visiting at the time, and my grandfather, a great baseball fan, showed up with him. It was a special Memorial Day game, and the seats were full. If I was ever going to do something remarkable, this was the moment to do it. I can remember catching sight of them in the wooden bleachers, my father in a white shirt with no tie and my grandfather wearing a white handkerchief on his bald head to protect him from the sun—the whole scene in my mind now drenched in this dazzling white light.

It probably goes without saying that I made a mess of it. I got no hits, lost my poise in the field, could not have been more nervous. Of all the hundreds of games I played during my childhood, this one was the worst.

Afterwards, walking to the car with my father, he told me I had played a nice game. No I hadn't, I said, it was terrible. Well, you did your best, he answered. You can't do well every time.

It was not that he was trying to encourage me. Nor was he trying to be unkind. Rather, he was saying what one says on such occasions, as if automatically. They were the right words to say, and yet they were delivered without feeling, an exercise in decorum, uttered in the same abstracted tone of voice he would use almost twenty years later when he said, "A beautiful baby. Good luck with it." I could see that his mind was some-where else.

In itself, this is not important. The important thing is this: I realized that even if I had done all the things I had hoped to do, his reaction would have been exactly the same. Whether I suc-ceeded or failed did not essentially matter to him. I was not de-fined for him by anything I did, but by what I was, and this meant that his perception of me would never change, that we were fixed in an unmoveable relationship, cut off from each other on opposite sides of a wall. Even more than that, I realized that none of this had anything to do with me. It had only to do with him. Like everything else in his life, he saw me only through the mists of his solitude, as if at several removes from himself. The world was a distant place for him, I think, a place he was never truly able to enter, and out there in the distance, among all the shadows that flitted past him, I was born, became his son, and grew up, as if I were just one more shadow, appearing and disappearing in a half-lit realm of his consciousness.

With his daughter, born when I was three and a half, it was somewhat easier for him. But in the end it was infinitely more difficult.

She was a beautiful child. Uncommonly fragile, with great brown eyes that would collapse into tears at the slightest prompting. She spent much of her time alone, a tiny figure wan-dering through an imaginary land of elves and fairies, dancing on tiptoe in lace-trimmed ballerina costumes, singing in a voice loud enough to be heard only by herself. She was a miniature Ophelia, already doomed, it would seem, to a life of constant inner struggle. She made few friends, had trouble keeping up in school, and was harassed by self-doubts, even at a very young age, that turned the simplest routines into nightmares of anguish and defeat. There were tantrums, fits of terrible crying, constant upheavals. Nothing ever seemed to go well for very long.

More sensitive to the nuances of the unhappy marriage around us than I was, her insecurity became monumental, crip-pling. At least once a day she would ask our mother if "she loved daddy." The answer was always the same: Of course I do.

It could not have been a very convincing lie. If it had been, there would not have been any need to ask the question again the next day.

On the other hand, it is difficult to see how the truth would have made things any better.

It was almost as if she gave off a scent of helplessness. One's immediate impulse was to protect her, to buffer her against the assaults of the world. Like everyone else, my father pampered her. The more she seemed to cry out for coddling, the more willing he was to give it to her. Long after she was able to walk, for example, he insisted on carrying her down the stairs. There is no question that he did it out of love, did it gladly because she was his little angel. But underneath this coddling was the implicit message that she would never be able to do anything for herself. She was not a person to him, but an angel, and because she was never compelled to act as an autonomous being, she could never become one.

My mother, however, saw what was happening. When my sister was five years old, she took her to an exploratory consultation with a child psychiatrist, and the doctor recommended that some form of therapy be started. That night, when my mother told my father the results of the meeting, he exploded in a violent rage. No daughter of mine, etc. The idea that his daughter needed psychiatric help was no different from being told she was a leper. He would not accept it. He would not even discuss it.

This is the point I am trying to make. His refusal to look into himself was matched by an equally stubborn refusal to look at the world, to accept even the most incontrovertible evidence it thrust under his nose. Again and again throughout his life he would stare a thing in the face, nod his head, and then turn around and say it was not there. It made conversation with him almost impossible. By the time you had managed to establish a common ground with him, he would take out his shovel and dig it out from under your feet.

Years later, when my sister suffered through a series of debilitating mental breakdowns, my father continued to believe there was nothing wrong with her. It was as though he were biologically unable to recognize her condition.

In one of his books R.D. Laing describes the father of a catatonic girl who on each visit to her in the hospital would grab her by the shoulders and shake her as hard as he could, telling her to "snap out of it." My father did not grab hold of my sister, but his attitude was essentially the same. What she needs, he would say, is to get a job, to clean herself up, to start living in the real world. Of course she did. But that was exactly what she could not do. She's just sensitive, he would say, she needs to overcome her shyness. By domesticating the problem to a quirk of personality, he could go on believing there was nothing wrong. It was not blindness so much as a failure of imagination. At what moment does a house stop being a house? When the roof is taken off? When the windows are removed? When the walls are knocked down? At what moment does it become a pile of rubble? She's just different, he would say, there's nothing wrong with her. And then one day the walls of your house finally collapse. If the door is still standing, however, all you have to do is walk through it, and you are back inside. It's pleasant sleeping out under the stars. Never mind the rain. It can't last very long.

Little by little, as the situation continued to get worse, he had to begin to accept it. But even then, at each stage along the way, his acceptance was unorthodox, taking on eccentric, almost self-nullifying forms. He became convinced, for example, that the one thing that could help her was a crash program in megavitamin therapy. This was the chemical approach to mental illness. Although it has never been proven to be an effective cure, this method of treatment has quite a large following. One can see why it would have attracted my father. Instead of having to wrestle with a devastating emotional fact, he could look upon the disease as a physical flaw, something that could be cured in the same way you cure the flu. The disease became an external force, a kind of bug that could be eradicated with an equal and opposite external force. In his eyes my sister was able to remain curiously untouched by all this. She was merely the *site* where the battle would take place, which meant that everything that was happening did not really affect *her*.

He spent several months trying to persuade her to begin this megavitamin program—even going so far as to take the pills himself, in order to prove that she would not be poisoned—and when at last she gave in, she did not take the pills for more than a week or two. The vitamins were expensive, but he did not balk at spending the money. On the other hand, he angrily resisted paying for other kinds of treatment. He did not believe that a stranger could possibly care about what happened to her. Psychiatrists were all charlatans, interested only in soaking their patients and driving fancy cars. He refused to pay the bills, which limited her to the shabbiest kind of public care. She was a pauper, with no income of her own, but he sent her almost nothing.

He was more than willing to take things into his own hands, however. Although it could not benefit either one of them, he wanted her to live in his house so that he could be the one responsible for looking after her. At least he could trust his own feelings, and he knew that he cared. But then, when she did come (for a few months, following one of her stays in the hospital), he did not disrupt his normal routine to accommodate her—but continued to spend most of his time out, leaving her to rattle around the enormous house like a ghost.

He was negligent and stubborn. But still, underneath it all, I know he suffered. Sometimes, on the phone, when he and I were discussing my sister, I could hear his voice break ever so slightly, as if he were trying to muffle a sob. Unlike everything else he ever came up against, my sister's illness finally *moved him*—but only to leave him with a feeling of utter helplessness. There is no greater sorrow for a parent than this helplessness. You have to accept it, even if you can't. And the more you accept it, the greater your despair becomes.

His despair became very great.

Wandering through the house today, without purpose, depressed, feeling that I have begun to lose touch with what I am writing, I chanced upon these words from a letter by Van

Gogh: "Like everyone else, I feel the need of family and friendship, affection and friendly intercourse. I am not made of stone or iron, like a hydrant or a lamp-post."

Perhaps this is what really counts: to arrive at the core of human feeling, in spite of the evidence.

These tiniest of images: incorrigible, lodged in the mud of memory, neither buried nor wholly retrievable. And yet each one, in itself, a fleeting resurrection, a moment otherwise lost. The way he walked, for example, weirdly balanced, bouncing on the balls of his feet, as if he were about to pitch forward, blindly, into the unknown. Or the way he hunched over the table as he ate, his shoulders tensed, always merely consuming the food, never savoring it. Or else the smells that emanated from the cars he used for work: fumes, leaking oil, exhaust; the clutter of cold metal tools; the constant rattle as the car moved. A memory of the day I went driving with him through downtown Newark, no more than six years old, and he slammed down on the brakes, the jolt of it flinging my head against the dashboard: the sudden swarm of black people around the car to see if I was all right, especially the woman who thrust a vanilla ice cream cone at me through the open window, and my saying "no thank you," very politely, too stunned to know what I really wanted. Or else another day in another car, some years later, when my father spat out the window only to realize that the window had not been lowered, and my boundless, irrational delight at seeing the saliva slither down the glass. And still, as a little boy, how he would sometimes take me with him to Jewish restaurants in neighborhoods I had never seen before, dark places filled with old people, each table graced with a tinted blue seltzer bottle, and how I would grow queasy, leave my food untouched, and content myself with watching him wolf down borscht, pirogen, and boiled meats covered with horse radish. I, who was being brought up as an American boy, who knew less about my ancestors than I did about Hopalong Cassidy's hat. Or how, when I was twelve or thirteen, and wanted desperately to go somewhere with a couple of my friends, I called him at work to get his permission, and he said to me, at a loss, not knowing how to put it, "You're just a bunch of green-horns," and how, for years afterward, my friends and I (one of them now dead, of a heroin overdose) would repeat those words as a piece of folklore, a nostalgic joke.

The size of his hands. Their callusses.
Eating the skin off the top of hot chocolate.
Tea with lemon.
The pairs of black, horn-rimmed glasses scattered through the house: on kitchen counters, on table tops, at the edge of the bathroom sink—always open, lying there like some strange, un-classified form of animal.
Watching him play tennis.
The way his knees sometimes buckled when he walked.
His face.
His resemblance to Abraham Lincoln, and how people al-ways remarked on it.
His fearlessness with dogs.
His face. And again, his face.
Tropical fish.

Often, he seemed to lose his concentration, to forget where he was, as if he had lost the sense of his own continuity. It made him accident prone: smashed thumbnails from using a hammer, numerous little accidents in the car.

His absent-mindedness as a driver: to the point that it some-times became frightening. I always thought it would be a car that did him in.

Otherwise, his health was so good that he seemed invulnera-ble, exempt from the physical ills that strike all the rest of us. As though nothing could ever touch him.

The way he spoke: as if making a great effort to rise up out of his solitude, as if his voice were rusty, had lost the habit of speaking. He always hemmed and hawed a lot, cleared his throat, seemed to sputter in mid-sentence. You felt, very defi-nitely, that he was uncomfortable.

In the same way, it always amused me as a child to watch him sign his name. He could not simply put the pen against the paper and write. As if unconsciously delaying the moment of truth, he would always make a slight, preliminary flourish, a circular movement an inch or two off the page, like a fly buzzing in the air and zeroing in on its spot, before he could get down to business. It was a modified version of the way Art Carney's Norton used to sign his name on *The Honeymooners*.

He even pronounced his words a little oddly. "Upown," for example, instead of "upon," as if the flourish of his hand had its counterpart in his voice. There was a musical, airy quality to it. Whenever he answered the phone, it was a lilting "hel-looo" that greeted you. The effect was not so much funny as endearing. It made him seem slightly daft, as if he were out of phase with the rest of the world—but not by much. Just a degree or two.

Indelible tics.

In those crazy, tensed-up moods he sometimes got into, he would always come out with bizarre opinions, not really taking them seriously, but happy to play devil's advocate in order to keep things lively. Teasing people put him in buoyant spirits, and after a particularly inane remark to someone he would often squeeze that person's leg—in a spot that always tickled. He literally liked to pull your leg.

Again the house.

No matter how negligent his care of it might have seemed from the outside, he believed in his system. Like a mad inventor protecting the secret of his perpetual motion machine, he would suffer no one to tamper with it. Once, when my wife and I were between apartments, we stayed in his house for three or four weeks. Finding the darkness of the house oppressive, we raised all the shades to let in the daylight. When my father returned home from work and saw what we had done, he flew into an uncontrollable rage, far out of proportion to any offense that might have been committed.

Anger of this sort rarely came out of him—only when he felt himself cornered, impinged upon, crushed by the presences of

others. Money questions sometimes triggered it off. Or else
some minor detail: the shades of his house, a broken plate, a little nothing at all.

Nevertheless, this anger was inside him—I believe constantly.
Like the house that was well ordered and yet falling apart from
within, the man himself was calm, almost supernatural in his
imperturbability, and yet prey to a roiling, unstoppable force of
fury within. All his life he strove to avoid a confrontation with
this force, nurturing a kind of automatic behavior that would
allow him to pass to the side of it. Reliance on fixed routines
freed him from the necessity of looking into himself when decisions had to be made; the cliché was always quick to come to
his lips ("A beautiful baby. Good luck with it") instead of
words he had gone out and looked for. All this tended to flatten
him out as a personality. But at the same time, it was also what
saved him, the thing that allowed him to live. To the extent that
he was able to live.

From a bag of loose pictures: a trick photograph taken in an
Atlantic City studio sometime during the Forties. There are several of him sitting around a table, each image shot from a different angle, so that at first you think it must be a group of
several different men. Because of the gloom that surrounds
them, because of the utter stillness of their poses, it looks as if
they have gathered there to conduct a seance. And then, as you
study the picture, you begin to realize that all these men are the
same man. The seance becomes a real seance, and it is as if he
has come there only to invoke himself, to bring himself back
from the dead, as if, by multiplying himself, he had inadvertently made himself disappear. There are five of him there, and
yet the nature of the trick photography denies the possibility of
eye contact among the various selves. Each one is condemned
to go on staring into space, as if under the gaze of the others,
but seeing nothing, never able to see anything. It is a picture of
death, a portrait of an invisible man.

Slowly, I am coming to understand the absurdity of the task I
have set for myself. I have a sense of trying to go somewhere, as

if I knew what I wanted to say, but the farther I go the more certain I am that the path toward my object does not exist. I have to invent the road with each step, and this means that I can never be sure of where I am. A feeling of moving around in circles, of perpetual back-tracking, of going off in many directions at once. And even if I do manage to make some progress, I am not at all convinced that it will take me to where I think I am going. Just because you wander in the desert, it does not mean there is a promised land.

When I first started, I thought it would come spontaneously, in a trance-like outpouring. So great was my need to write that I thought the story would be written by itself. But the words have come very slowly so far. Even on the best days I have not been able to write more than a page or two. I seem to be afflicted, cursed by some failure of mind to concentrate on what I am doing. Again and again I have watched my thoughts trail off from the thing in front of me. No sooner have I thought one thing than it evokes another thing, and then another thing, until there is an accumulation of detail so dense that I feel I am going to suffocate. Never before have I been so aware of the rift between thinking and writing. For the past few days, in fact, I have begun to feel that the story I am trying to tell is somehow incompatible with language, that the degree to which it resists language is an exact measure of how closely I have come to saying something important, and that when the moment arrives for me to say the one truly important thing (assuming it exists), I will not be able to say it.

There has been a wound, and I realize now that it is very deep. Instead of healing me as I thought it would, the act of writing has kept this wound open. At times I have even felt the pain of it concentrated in my right hand, as if each time I picked up the pen and pressed it against the page, my hand were being torn apart. Instead of burying my father for me, these words have kept him alive, perhaps more so than ever. I not only see him as he was, but as he is, as he will be, and each day he is there, invading my thoughts, stealing up on me without warning: lying in the coffin underground, his body still intact, his fingernails and hair continuing to grow. A feeling that

if I am to understand anything, I must penetrate this image of darkness, that I must enter the absolute darkness of earth.

Kenosha, Wisconsin. 1911 or 1912. Not even he was sure of the date. In the confusion of a large, immigrant family, birth records could not have been considered very important. What matters is that he was the last of five surviving children—a girl and four boys, all born within a span of eight years—and that his mother, a tiny, ferocious woman who could barely speak English, held the family together. She was the matriarch, the absolute dictator, the prime mover who stood at the center of the universe.

His father died in 1919, which meant that except for his earliest childhood he had no father. During my own childhood he told me three different stories about his father's death. In one version, he had been killed in a hunting accident. In another, he had fallen off a ladder. In the third, he had been shot down during the First World War. I knew these contradictions made no sense, but I assumed this meant that not even my father knew the facts. Because he had been so young when it happened— only seven—I figured that he had never been given the exact story. But then, this made no sense either. One of his brothers surely would have told him.

All my cousins, however, told me that they, too, had been given different explanations by their fathers.

No one ever talked about my grandfather. Until a few years ago, I had never seen a picture of him. It was as though the family had decided to pretend he had never existed.

Among the photographs I found in my father's house last month there was one family portrait from those early days in Kenosha. All the children are there. My father, no more than a year old, is sitting on his mother's lap, and the other four are standing around her in the tall, uncut grass. There are two trees behind them and a large wooden house behind the trees. A whole world seems to emerge from this portrait: a distinct time, a distinct place, an indestructible sense of the past. The first time I looked at the picture, I noticed that it had been torn down the middle and then clumsily mended, leaving one

of the trees in the background hanging eerily in mid-air. I assumed the picture had been torn by accident and thought no more about it. The second time I looked at it, however, I studied this tear more closely and discovered things I must have been blind to miss before. I saw a man's fingertips grasping the torso of one of my uncles; I saw, very distinctly, that another of my uncles was not resting his hand on his brother's back, as I had first thought, but against a chair that was not there. And then I realized what was strange about the picture: my grandfather had been cut out of it. The image was distorted because part of it had been eliminated. My grandfather had been sitting in a chair next to his wife with one of his sons standing between his knees—and he was not there. Only his fingertips remained: as if he were trying to crawl back into the picture from some hole deep in time, as if he had been exiled to another dimension.

The whole thing made me shake.

I learned the story of my grandfather's death some time ago. If not for an extraordinary coincidence, it never would have become known.

In 1970 one of my cousins went to Europe on a vacation with her husband. On the plane she found herself sitting next to an old man and, as people often do, they struck up a conversation to pass the time. It turned out that his man lived in Kenosha, Wisconsin. My cousin was amused by the coincidence and remarked that her father had lived there as a boy. Out of curiosity, the man asked her the name of her family. When she told him Auster, he turned pale. Auster? Your grandmother wasn't a crazy little woman with red hair, was she? Yes, that was my grandmother, my cousin answered. A crazy little woman with red hair.

And then he told her the story. It had happened more than fifty years before, and yet he still remembered the important details.

When this man returned home from his vacation, he tracked down the newspaper articles connected with the story, had them photocopied, and sent them to my cousin. This was his cover letter:

June 15, 70

Dear —— and ——

It was good to get your letter, and altho it did look like the task might be complicated, I had a stroke of luck.—Fran and I went out to dinner with a Fred Plons and his wife, and it was Fred's father who had bought the apartment bldg on Park Ave from your family.—Mr. Plons is about three years younger than myself, but he claimed that the case (at that time) fascinated him and he remembered quite a few details.—He stated that your grandfather was the first person to be buried in the Jewish Cemetery here in Kenosha.—(Previous to 1919 the Jewish people had no cemetery in Kenosha, but had their loved ones buried either in Chicago or Milwaukee.) With this information, I had no trouble locating the plot where your grandfather is buried.—And I was able to pin point the date. The rest is in the copy I am forwarding to you.—

I only ask that your father should never learn of this knowledge that I am passing on to you—I would not want him to have any more grief than he already has suffered . . .

I hope that this will shed some light on your Father's actions over the past years.

Our fondest regards to you both—
Ken & Fran

The newspaper articles are sitting on my desk. Now that the moment has come to write about them; I am surprised to find myself doing everything I can to put it off. All morning I have procrastinated. I have taken the trash to the dump. I have played with Daniel in the yard for almost an hour. I have read the entire newspaper—right down to the line scores of the spring training baseball games. Even now, as I write about my reluctance to write, I find myself impossibly restless: after every few words I pop up from my chair, pace the floor, listen to the wind outside as it bangs the loose gutters against the house. The least thing is able to distract me.

It is not that I am afraid of the truth. I am not even afraid to say it. My grandmother murdered my grandfather. On January 23, 1919, precisely sixty years before my father died, his mother shot and killed his father in the kitchen of their house on Fremont Avenue in Kenosha, Wisconsin. The facts themselves do not disturb me any more than might be expected. The difficult thing is to see them in print—unburied, so to speak, from the realm of secrets and turned into a public event. There are more than twenty articles, most of them long, all of them from the *Kenosha Evening News*. Even in this barely legible state, almost totally obscured by age and the hazards of photocopying, they still have the ability to shock. I assume they are typical of the journalism of the time, but that does not make them any less sensational. They are a mixture of scandalmongering and sentimentality, heightened by the fact that the people involved were Jews—and therefore strange, almost by definition—which gives the whole account a leering, condescending tone. And yet, granted the flaws in style, the facts seem to be there. I do not think they explain everything, but there is no question that they explain a great deal. A boy cannot live through this kind of thing without being affected by it as a man.

In the margins of these articles, I can just manage to decipher some of the smaller news stories of that time, events that were relegated to near insignificance in comparison to the murder. For example: the recovery of Rosa Luxemburg's body from the Landwehr Canal. For example: the Versailles peace conference. And on and on, day after day, through the following: the Eugene Debs case; a note on Caruso's first film ("The situations . . . are said to be highly dramatic and filled with stirring heart appeal"); battle reports from the Russian Civil War; the funerals of Karl Liebnecht and thirty-one other Spartacists ("More than fifty thousand persons marched in the procession which was five miles long. Fully twenty percent of these bore wreaths. There was no shouting or cheering"); the ratification of the national prohibition amendment ("William Jennings Bryan—the man who made grape juice famous—was there

with a broad smile"); the textile strike in Lawrence, Massachusetts, led by the Wobblies; the death of Emiliano Zapata,
"bandit leader in southern Mexico"; Winston Churchill; Bela
Kun; Premier Lenine (sic); Woodrow Wilson; Dempsey versus
Willard.

I have read through the articles about the murder a dozen
times. Still, I find it hard to believe that I did not dream them.
They loom up at me with all the force of a trick of the unconscious, distorting reality in the same way dreams do. Because
the huge headlines announcing the murder dwarf everything
else that happened in the world that day, they give the event the
same egocentric importance we give to the things that happen
in our private lives. It is almost like the drawing a child makes
when he is troubled by some inexpressible fear: the most important thing is always the biggest thing. Perspective is lost in
favor of proportion—which is dictated not by the eye but by
the demands of the mind.

I read these articles as history. But also as a cave drawing discovered on the inner walls of my own skull.

The headlines on the first day, January 24, cover more than a
third of the front page.

HARRY AUSTER KILLED
WIFE HELD BY POLICE

———

Former Prominent Real Estate Operator is Shot to Death
in the Kitchen of the Home of His Wife
On Thursday Night Following a Family
Wrangle Over Money—and a Woman.

———

WIFE SAYS HUSBAND WAS A SUICIDE

———

Dead Man Had Bullet Wound in His Neck and in the Left Hip
and Wife Admits That Revolver With Which the Shooting Was
Done Was Her Property—Nine-Year-Old Son, Witness of the
Tragedy, May Hold Solution to the Mystery.

———

According to the newspaper, "Auster and his wife had separated some time ago and an action for divorce was pending in the Circuit Court for Kenosha county. They had had trouble on several occasions over money. They had also quarreled over the fact that Auster [illegible] friendly with a young woman known to the wife as 'Fanny.' It is believed that 'Fanny' figured in the trouble between Auster and his wife immediately preceding the shooting. . . ."

Because my grandmother did not confess until the twenty-eighth, there was some confusion about what really happened. My grandfather (who was thirty-six years old) arrived at the house at six o'clock in the evening with "suits of clothing" for his two oldest sons "while it was stated by witnesses Mrs. Auster was in the bedroom putting Sam, the youngest boy, into bed. Sam [my father] declared that he did not see his mother take a revolver from under the mattress as he was tucked into bed for the night."

It seems that my grandfather had then gone into the kitchen to repair an electric switch and that one of my uncles (the second youngest son) had held a candle for him to see by. "The boy declared that he became panic stricken when he heard the shot and saw a flash of a revolver and fled the room." According to my grandmother, her husband had shot himself. She admitted they had been arguing about money, and "then he said, she continued, 'there is going to be an end for you or me,' and he threatened me. I did not know he had the revolver. I had kept it under the mattress of my bed and he knew it."

Since my grandmother spoke almost no English, I assume that this statement, and all others attributed to her, was invented by the reporter. Whatever it was she said, the police did not believe her. "Mrs. Auster repeated her story to the various police officers without making any decided change in it and she professed great surprise when she was told that she was to be held by the police. With a great deal of tenderness she kissed little Sam good night and then went off to the county jail.

"The two Auster boys were guests of the police department last night sleeping in the squad room and this morning the boys were apparently entirely recovered from any fright they had suffered as a result of the tragedy at their home."

Toward the end of the article, this information is given about my grandfather. "Harry Auster was a native of Austria. He came to this country a number of years ago and had resided in Chicago, in Canada, and in Kenosha. He and his wife, according to the story told the police, later returned to Austria but she rejoined her husband in this country about the time they came to Kenosha. Auster bought a number of homes in the second ward and for some time his operations were on a large scale. He built the big triple flat building on South Park avenue and another one known as the Auster flats on South Exchange street. Six or eight months ago he met with financial reverses. . . .

"Some time ago Mrs. Auster appealed to the police to aid her in watching Mr. Auster as she alleged that he had relations with a young woman which she believed should be investigated. It was in this way that the police first learned of the woman 'Fanny'. . . .

"Many people had seen and talked with Auster on Thursday afternoon and these people all declared that he appeared to be normal and that he showed no signs of desiring to take his own life. . . ."

The next day was the coroner's inquest. My uncle, as the only witness to the incident, was called on to testify. "A sad-eyed little boy, nervously twirling his stocking cap, wrote the second chapter in the Auster murder mystery Friday afternoon. . . . His attempts to save the family name were tragically pathetic. Again and again when asked if his parents were quarrelling he would answer 'They were just talking' until at last, apparently remembering his oath, he added 'and maybe quarrelling—well just a little bit.' " The article describes the jurors as "weirdly stirred by the boy's efforts to shield both his father and his mother."

The idea of suicide was clearly not going to wash. In the last paragraph the reporter writes that "developments of a startling nature have been hinted by officials."

Then came the funeral. It gave the anonymous reporter an opportunity to emulate some of the choicest diction of Victorian melodrama. By now the murder was no longer merely a scandal. It had been turned into a stirring entertainment.

WIDOW TEARLESS AT AUSTER GRAVE

Mrs. Anna Auster Under Guard Attends Funeral of
Husband, Harry Auster, Sunday.

"Dry-eyed and without the least sign of emotion or grief, Mrs. Harry Auster, who is held here in connection with the mysterious death of her husband, Harry Auster, attended Sunday morning, under guard, the funeral services of the man, in connection with whose death she is being held.

"Neither at the Crossin Chapel, where she looked for the first time since Thursday night upon the dead face of her husband nor at the burial ground did she show the least sign of weakening. The only intimation which she gave of breaking under the terrific strain of the ordeal was when over the grave, after the obsequies were finished, she asked for a conference this afternoon with the Rev. M. Hartman, pastor of the B'nai Zadek Congregation. . . .

"When the rites were completed Mrs. Auster calmly tightened the fox fur collar more closely about her throat and signified to the police that she was ready to leave. . . .

"After short ritualistic ceremonies the funeral procession was formed on Wisconsin street. Mrs. Auster asked that she also be allowed to go to the burial ground and the request was granted readily by the police. She seemed very petulant over the fact that no carriage had been provided for her, perhaps remembering that short season of apparent wealth when the Auster limousine was seen in Kenosha. . . .

". . . The ordeal was made exceptionally long because some delay had occurred in the preparation of the grave and while she waited she called Sam, the youngest boy, to her, and tucked his coat collar more closely around his neck. She spoke quietly to him but with this exception she was silent until after the rites were finished. . . .

"A prominent figure at the funeral was Samuel Auster, of De-troit, the brother of Harry Auster. He took as his especial care the younger children and attempted to console them in their grief.

"In speeches and demonstrations Auster appeared very bitter about his brother's death. He showed clearly that he disbelieved the theory of suicide and uttered remarks which savoured of accusations of the widow. . . .

"The Rev. M. Hartman . . . preached an eloquent sermon at the grave. He lamented the fact that the first person to be buried in the new cemetery should be one who had died by violence and who had been killed in his prime. He paid tribute to the enterprise of Harry Auster but deplored his early death.

"The widow appeared to be unmoved by the tributes paid to her dead husband. She indifferently opened her coat to allow the patriarch to cut a gash in her knitted sweater, a token of grief prescribed by the Hebrew faith.

"Officials in Kenosha fail to give up the suspicion that Auster was killed by his wife. . . ."

The paper of the following day, January 26th, carried the news of the confession. After her meeting with the rabbi, she had requested a conference with the chief of police. "When she entered the room she trembled a little and was plainly agitated as the chief provided a chair. 'You know what your little boy told us,' the latter began when he realized that the psychological moment had come. 'You don't want us to think that he's lying to us, do you?' And the mother, whose face has been for days so masked as to reveal nothing of the horror hidden behind it, tore off the camouflage, became suddenly tender, and sobbed out her awful secret. 'He isn't lying to you at all; everything he has said is true. I shot him and I want to make a confession.' "

This was her formal statement: "My name is Anna Auster. I shot Harry Auster at the city of Kenosha, Wisconsin on the 23rd day of January A.D. 1919. I have heard people remark that three shots were fired, but I do not remember how many shots were fired that day. My reason for shooting the said

Harry Auster is on account of the fact that he, the said Harry Auster, abused me. I was just like crazy when I shot the said Harry Auster. I never thought of shooting him, the said Harry Auster, until the moment I shot him. I think that this is the gun I shot the said Harry Auster with. I make this statement of my own free will and without being forced to do so."

The reporter continues, "On the table before Mrs. Auster lay the revolver with which her husband was shot to death. As she spoke of it she touched it falteringly and then drew her hand back with a noticeable tremor of horror. Without speaking the chief laid the gun aside and asked Mrs. Auster if there was more she cared to say.

" 'That's all for now,' " she replied composedly. 'You sign it for me and I'll make my mark.'

"Her orders—for a little moment she was almost regal again—were obeyed, she acknowledged the signature, and asked to be returned to her cell . . ."

At the arraignment the next day a plea of not guilty was entered by her attorney. "Muffled in a plush coat and a boa of fox fur, Mrs. Auster entered the court room. . . . She smiled at a friend in the crowd as she took her seat before the desk."

By the reporter's own admission, the hearing was "uneventful." But still, he could not resist making this observation: "An incident occurred upon her return to her barred room which furnished a commentary on Mrs. Auster's state of mind.

"A woman, held on a charge of association with a married man, had been brought to the jail for incarceration in an adjoining cell. Upon seeing her, Mrs. Auster asked about the newcomer and learned the particulars in the case.

" 'She ought to get ten years,' she said as the iron door clanged pitilessly. 'It was one of her kind that put me here.' "

After some intricate legal discussions concerning bail that were elaborately reported for the next few days, she was set free. " 'Have you any notion that this woman will not appear for trial?' the court asked the attorneys. It was attorney Baker who answered: 'Where could a woman with five children like these go? She clings to them and the court can see that they cling to her.' "

For a week the press was quiet. Then, on February 8th, there was a story about "the active support that the cause is being given by some of the papers published in the Jewish language in Chicago. Some of these papers contained columns arguing the case of Mrs. Auster and it is declared that these articles have strongly urged her defense . . .

"Friday afternoon Mrs. Auster with one of her children sat in the office of her attorney while portions of these articles were read. She sobbed like a child as the interpreter read to the attorney the contents of these papers . . .

"Attorney Baker declared this morning that the defense of Mrs. Auster would be one of emotional insanity . . .

"It is expected that the trial of Mrs. Auster will be one of the most interesting murder trials ever tried in the Circuit Court for Kenosha county and the human interest story that has been featured in the defense of the woman up to this time is expected to be largely developed at the trial."

Then nothing for a month. On March 10th the headlines read:

ANNA AUSTER TRIED SUICIDE

The suicide attempt had taken place in Peterboro, Ontario in 1910—by taking carbolic acid and then turning on the gas. The attorney brought this information before the court in order to be granted a delay in the trial so that he would have enough time to secure affidavits. "Attorney Baker held that at the same time the woman had endangered the lives of two of her children and that the story of the attempted suicide was important in that it would show the mental condition of Mrs. Auster."

March 27th. The trial was set for April 7th. After that, another week of silence. And then, on April 4th, as if things had been getting just a bit too dull, a new development.

AUSTER SHOOTS BROTHER'S WIDOW

"Sam Auster, brother of Harry Auster . . . made an unsuccessful attempt to avenge the death of his brother just after ten o'clock this morning when he shot at Mrs. Auster. . . . The shooting occurred just outside the Miller Grocery Store. . . .

"Auster followed Mrs. Auster outside the door and fired once at her. Mrs. Auster, though she was not struck by the shot, fell to the sidewalk and Auster returned to the store declaring according to witnesses, 'Well, I'm glad I done that.' There he calmly awaited arrest. . . .

"At the police station . . . Auster, entirely broken down nervously, gave his explanation of the shooting.

" 'That woman,' he said, 'has killed my four brothers and my mother. I've tried to help but she won't let me.' Then as he was being led down to the cell, he sobbed out, 'God's going to take my part though, I know that.'

"At his cell Auster declared that he had tried everything within his power to help the children of his dead brother. The fact that the court had refused to appoint him administrator for the estate because they declared that the widow had some rights in the case had preyed on his mind recently. . . . 'She's no widow,' he commented on that incident this morning. 'She is a murderer and should have no rights. . . .'

"Auster will not be arraigned immediately in order to make a thorough investigation of the case. The police admit that the death of his brother and subsequent events may have so preyed on his mind that he was not entirely responsible for his deed. Auster expressed several times a hope that he should die too and every precaution is being taken to prevent him from taking his own life. . . ."

The next day's paper had this to add: "Auster spent a rather troublesome night in the city lockup. Several times the officers found him sobbing in the cell and he appeared to be hysterical. . . .

"It was admitted that Mrs. Auster had suffered from a 'bad case of nerves' as a result of the fright which had attended the attack on her life on Friday, but it was declared that she would be able to be in court when the case against her is called for trial on Monday evening."

After three days the state rested its case. Contending that the murder had been premeditated, the district attorney relied heavily on the testimony of a certain Mrs. Mathews, an employee at the Miller Grocery Store, who contended that "Mrs. Auster came to the store three times on the day of the shooting to use the telephone. On one of those occasions, the witness said, Mrs. Auster called up her husband and asked him to come to the house and fix a light. She said that Auster had promised to come at six o'clock."

But even if she invited him to the house, it does not mean that she intended to kill him once he was there.

It makes no difference anyway. Whatever the facts might have been, the defense attorney shrewdly turned everything to his own advantage. His strategy was to offer overwhelming evidence on two fronts: on the one hand, to prove infidelity on the part of my grandfather, and on the other, to demonstrate a history of mental instability on the part of my grandmother—the two of them combining to produce a case of justifiable homicide or homicide "by reason of insanity." Either one would do.

Attorney Baker's opening remarks were calculated to draw every possible ounce of sympathy from the jury. "He told how Mrs. Auster had toiled with her husband to build up the home and happiness which once was theirs in Kenosha after they had passed through years of hardships. . . . 'Then after they had labored together to build up this home,' continued Attorney Baker, 'there came this siren from the city and Anna Auster was cast aside like a rag. Instead of supplying food for his family, her husband kept Fanny Koplan in a flat in Chicago. The money which she had helped to accumulate was being lavished on a more beautiful woman and after such abuse is there any wonder that her mind was shattered and that for the moment she lost control of her senses.' "

The first witness for the defense was Mrs. Elizabeth Grossman, my grandmother's only sister, who lived on a farm near Brunswick, New Jersey. "She made a splendid witness. She told in a simple manner the whole story of the life of Mrs. Auster; of her birth in Austria; of the death of her mother when Mrs. Auster was but six years of age; of the trip with her sister to this country eight years later; of long hours served as a maker of hats and bonnets in New York millinery shops; of how by this work the immigrant girl accumulated a few hundred dollars. She told of the marriage of the woman to Auster just after she reached her twenty-third birthday and of their business ventures; of their failure in a little candy store and their long trip to Lawrence, Kas., where they attempted to start over and where——, the first child was born; of the return to New York and the second failure in business which ended in bankruptcy and the flight of Auster into Canada. She told of Mrs. Auster following Auster to Canada; of the desertion by Auster of the wife and little children and how he had said that he was 'going to make way with himself' [sic] and how he had told the wife that he was taking fifty dollars so that when he was dead it might be found on him and used to give him a decent burial. . . . She said that during their residence in Canada they were known as Mr. and Mrs. Harry Ball. . . .

"A little break in the story which could not be furnished by Mrs. Grossman, was furnished by former Chief Constable Archie Moore and Abraham Low, both of Peterboro county, Canada. These men told of the departure of Auster from Peterboro and the grief of his wife. Auster, they said, left Peterboro July 14, 1909, and the following night Moore found Mrs. Auster in a room of their shabby home suffering from the effects of gas. She and the children lay on a mattress on the floor while the gas was flowing from four open jets. Moore told of the further fact that he had found a vial of carbolic acid in the room and that traces of the acid had been found on the lips of Mrs. Auster. She was taken to a hospital, the witness declared, and was ill for many days. Both of these men declared that in their opinion there was no doubt but that Mrs. Auster showed signs of insanity at the time she attempted her life in Canada."

Further witnesses included the two oldest children, each of whom chronicled the family's domestic troubles. Much was said about Fanny, and also the frequent squabbles at home. "He

said that Auster had a habit of throwing dishes and glass ware
and that at one time his mother's arm had been so badly cut
that it was necessary to call a physician to attend her. He declared that his father used profane and indecent language toward his mother at these times. . . ."

Another witness from Chicago testified that she had frequently seen my grandmother beat her head against the wall in
fits of mental anguish. A police officer from Kenosha told how
at "one time he had seen Mrs. Auster running wildly down a
street. He stated that her hair was 'more or less' dishevelled and
added that she acted much like a woman who had lost her
mind." A doctor was also called in, and he contended that she
had been suffering from "acute mania."

My grandmother's testimony lasted three hours. "Between
stifled sobs and recourse to tears, she told the story of her life
with Auster up to the time of the 'accident'. . . . Mrs. Auster
stood the ordeal of cross questioning very well, and her story
was told over three times in almost the same way."

In his summation "Attorney Baker made a strong emotional
plea for the release of Mrs. Auster. In a speech lasting nearly an
hour and a half he retold in an eloquent manner the story of
Mrs. Auster. . . . Several times Mrs. Auster was moved to tears
by the statements of her attorney and women in the audience
were sobbing several times as the attorney painted the picture
of the struggling immigrant woman seeking to maintain their
home."

The judge gave the jury the option of only two verdicts: guilty
or innocent of murder. It took them less than two hours to make
their decision. As the bulletin of April 12th put it: "At four
thirty o'clock this afternoon the jury in the trial of Mrs. Anna
Auster returned a verdict finding the defendant not guilty."

April 14th. " 'I am happier now than I have been for seventeen
years,' said Mrs. Auster Saturday afternoon as she shook hands
with each of the jurors following the return of the verdict. 'As
long as Harry lived,' she said to one of them, 'I was worried. I
never knew real happiness. Now I regret that he had to die by
my hand. I am as happy now as I ever expect to be. . . .'

"As Mrs. Auster left the court room she was attended by her daughter . . . and the two younger children, who had waited patiently in the courtroom for the return of the verdict which freed their mother. . . .

"At the county jail Sam Auster . . . while he cannot understand it all, says he is willing to abide by the decision of the twelve jurors. . . .

" 'Last night when I heard of the verdict,' he said when interviewed on Sunday morning, 'I dropped on the floor. I could not believe that she could go clear free after killing my brother and her husband. It is all too big for me. I don't understand, but I shall let it go now. I tried once to settle it in my way and failed and I can't do anything now but accept what the court has said.' "

The next day he, too, was released. " 'I am going back to my work in the factory,' Auster told the District Attorney. 'Just as soon as I get money enough I am going to raise a head stone over the grave of my brother and then I am going to give my energies to the support of the children of one of my brothers who lived in Austria and who fell fighting in the Austrian army.'

"The conference this morning brought out the fact that Sam Auster is the last of the five Auster brothers. Three of the boys fought with the Austrian army in the world war and all of them fell in battle."

In the last paragraph of the last article about the case, the newspaper reports that "Mrs. Auster is now planning to take the children and leave for the east within a few days. . . . It was said that Mrs. Auster decided to take this action on the advice of her attorneys, who told her that she should go to some new home and start life without any one knowing the story of the trial."

It was, I suppose, a happy ending. At least for the newspaper readers of Kenosha, the clever Attorney Baker, and, no doubt, for my grandmother. Nothing further is said, of course, about the fortunes of the Auster family. The public record ends with this announcement of their departure for the east.

Because my father rarely spoke to me about the past, I learned very little about what followed. But from the few things he did mention, I was able to form a fairly good idea of the climate in which the family lived.

For example, they moved constantly. It was not uncommon for my father to attend two, or even three different schools in a single year. Because they had no money, life became a series of escapes from landlords and creditors. In a family that had already closed in on itself, this nomadism walled them off entirely. There were no enduring points of reference: no home, no town, no friends that could be counted on. Only the family itself. It was almost like living in quarantine.

My father was the baby, and for his whole life he continued to look up to his three older brothers. As a boy he was known as Sonny. He suffered from asthma and allergies, did well in school, played end on the football team and ran the 440 for the track team at Central High in Newark. He graduated in the first year of the Depression, went to law school at night for a semester or two, and then dropped out, exactly as his brothers had done before him.

The four brothers stuck together. There was something almost medieval about their loyalty to one another. Although they had their differences, in many ways did not even like one another, I think of them not as four separate individuals but as a clan, a quadruplicate image of solidarity. Three of them—the youngest three—wound up as business partners and lived in the same town, and the fourth, who lived only two towns away, had been set up in business by the other three. There was scarcely a day that my father did not see his brothers. And that means for his entire life: every day for more than sixty years.

They picked up habits from each other, figures of speech, little gestures, intermingling to such a degree that it was impossible to tell which one had been the source of any given attitude or idea. My father's feelings were unbending: he never said a word against any of his brothers. Again, it was the other defined not by what he did but by what he was. If one of the brothers happened to slight him or do something objectionable, my father would nevertheless refuse to pass judgment. He's my brother, he would say, as if that explained everything.

Brotherhood was the first principle, the unassailable postulate, the one and only article of faith. Like belief in God, to question it was heresy.

As the youngest, my father was the most loyal of the four and also the one least respected by the others. He worked the hardest, was the most generous to his nephews and nieces, and yet these things were never fully recognized, much less appreciated. My mother recalls that on the day of her wedding, at the party following the ceremony, one of the brothers actually propositioned her. Whether he would have carried through with the escapade is another matter. But the mere fact of teasing her like that gives a rough idea of how he felt about my father. You do not do that sort of thing on a man's wedding day, even if he is your brother.

At the center of the clan was my grandmother, a Jewish Mammy Yokum, a mother to end all mothers. Fierce, refractory, the boss. It was common loyalty to her that kept the brothers so close. Even as grown men, with wives and children of their own, they would faithfully go to her house every Friday night for dinner—without their families. This was the relationship that mattered, and it took precedence over everything else. There must have been something slightly comical about it: four big men, each one over six feet, waiting on a little old woman, more than a foot shorter than they were.

One of the few times they came with their wives, a neighbor happened to walk in and was surprised to find such a large gathering. Is this your family, Mrs. Auster? he asked. Yes, she answered, with great smiles of pride. This is —. This is —. This is —. And this is Sam. The neighbor was a little taken aback. And these lovely ladies, he asked. Who are they? Oh, she answered with a casual wave of the hand. That's —'s. That's —'s. That's —'s. And that's Sam's.

The picture painted of her in the Kenosha newspaper was by no means inaccurate. She lived for her children. (Attorney Baker: Where could a woman with five children like these go? She clings to them and the court can see that they cling to her.) At the same time, she was a tyrant, given to screaming and hysterical fits.

When she was angry, she would beat her sons over the head with a broom. She demanded allegiance, and she got it.

Once, when my father had saved the huge sum of ten or twenty dollars from his newspaper route to buy himself a new bicycle, his mother walked into the room, cracked open his piggy bank, and took the money from him without so much as an apology. She needed the money to pay some bills, and my father had no recourse, no way to air his grievance. When he told me this story his object was not to show how his mother wronged him, but to demonstrate how the good of the family was always more important than the good of any of its members. He might have been unhappy, but he did not complain.

This was rule by caprice. For a child, it meant that the sky could fall on top of him at any moment, that he could never be sure of anything. Therefore, he learned never to trust anyone. Not even himself. Someone would always come along to prove that what he thought was wrong, that it did not count for anything. He learned never to want anything too much.

My father lived with his mother until he was older than I am now. He was the last one to go off on his own, the one who had been left behind to take care of her. It would be wrong to say, however, that he was a mother's boy. He was too independent, had been too fully indoctrinated into the ways of manhood by his brothers. He was good to her, was dutiful and considerate, but not without a certain distance, even humor. After he was married, she called him often, haranguing him about this and that. My father would put the receiver down on the table, walk to the other end of the room and busy himself with some chore for a few minutes, then return to the phone, pick it up, say something innocuous to let her know he was there (uh-huh, uh-huh, mmmmmm, that's right), and then wander off again, back and forth, until she had talked herself out.

The comical side of his obtuseness. And sometimes it served him very well.

I remember a tiny, shriveled creature sitting in the front parlor of a two-family house in the Weequahic section of Newark reading

the *Jewish Daily Forward*. Although I knew I would have to do it
whenever I saw her, it made me cringe to kiss her. Her face was so
wrinkled, her skin so inhumanly soft. Worse than that was her
smell—a smell I was much later able to identify as that of cam-
phor, which she must have put in her bureau drawers and which,
over the years, had seeped into the fabric of her clothes. This
odor was inseparable in my mind from the idea of "grandma."

As far as I can remember, she took virtually no interest in
me. The one time she gave me a present, it was a second- or
third-hand children's book, a biography of Benjamin Franklin.
I remember reading it all the way through and can even recall
some of the episodes. Franklin's future wife, for example, laugh-
ing at him the first time she saw him—walking through the
streets of Philadelphia with an enormous loaf of bread under
his arm. The book had a blue cover and was illustrated with sil-
houettes. I must have been seven or eight at the time.

After my father died, I discovered a trunk that had once belonged to his mother in the cellar of his house. It was locked,
and I decided to force it open with a hammer and screwdriver,
thinking it might contain some buried secret, some long lost
treasure. As the hasp fell down and I raised the lid, there it was,
all over again—that smell, wafting up toward me, immediate,
palpable, as if it had been my grandmother herself. I felt as
though I had just opened her coffin.

There was nothing of interest in it: a set of carving knives, a
heap of imitation jewelry. Also a hard plastic dress-up pocket-
book, a kind of octagonal box with a handle on it. I gave the
thing to Daniel, and he immediately started using it as a
portable garage for his fleet of little trucks and cars.

My father worked hard all his life. At nine he had his first job.
At eighteen he had a radio repair business with one of his
brothers. Except for a brief moment when he was hired as an
assistant in Thomas Edison's laboratory (only to have the job
taken away from him the next day because Edison learned he
was a Jew), my father never worked for anyone but himself. He
was a very demanding boss, far more exacting than any
stranger could have been.

The radio shop eventually led to a small appliance store, which in turn led to a large furniture store. From there he began to dabble in real estate (buying, for example, a house for his mother to live in), until this gradually displaced the store as the focus of his attention and became a business in its own right. The partnership with two of his brothers carried over from one thing to the next.

Up early every morning, home late at night, and in between, work, nothing but work. Work was the name of the country he lived in, and he was one of its greatest patriots. That is not to say, however, that work was pleasure for him. He worked hard because he wanted to earn as much money as possible. Work was a means to an end—a means to money. But the end was not something that could bring him pleasure either. As the young Marx wrote: "If *money* is the bond binding me to *human life*, binding society to me, binding me and nature and man, is not money the bond of all *bonds*? Can it not dissolve and bind all ties? Is it not, therefore, the universal *agent of separation*?"

He dreamed all his life of becoming a millionaire, of being the richest man in the world. It was not so much the money itself he wanted, but what it represented: not merely success in the eyes of the world, but a way of making himself untouchable. Having money means more than being able to buy things: it means that the world need never affect you. Money in the sense of protection, then, not pleasure. Having been without money as a child, and therefore vulnerable to the whims of the world, the idea of wealth became synonymous for him with the idea of escape: from harm, from suffering, from being a victim. He was not trying to buy happiness, but simply an absence of unhappiness. Money was the panacea, the objectification of his deepest, most inexpressible desires as a human being. He did not want to spend it, he wanted to have it, to know that it was there. Money not as an elixir, then, but as an antidote: the small vial of medicine you carry in your pocket when you go out into the jungle—just in case you are bitten by a poisonous snake.

At times, his reluctance to spend money was so great it almost resembled a disease. It never came to such a point that he would deny himself what he needed (for his needs were minimal), but more subtly, each time he had to buy something, he would opt for the cheapest solution. This was bargain shopping as a way of life.

Implicit in this attitude was a kind of perceptual primitivism. All distinctions were eliminated, everything was reduced to its least common denominator. Meat was meat, shoes were shoes, a pen was a pen. It did not matter that you could choose between chuck and porterhouse, that there were throwaway ball points for thirty-nine cents and fifty-dollar fountain pens that would last for twenty years. The truly fine object was almost to be abhorred: it meant that you would have to pay an extravagant price, and that made it morally unsound. On a more general level, this translated itself into a permanent state of sensory deprivation: by closing his eyes to so much, he denied himself intimate contact with the shapes and textures of the world, cut himself off from the possibility of experiencing aesthetic pleasure. The world he looked out on was a practical place. Each thing in it had a value and a price, and the idea was to get the things you needed at a price that was as close to the value as possible. Each thing was understood only in terms of its function, judged only by how much it cost, never as an intrinsic object with its own special properties. In some way, I imagine it must have made the world seem a dull place to him. Uniform, colorless, without depth. If you see the world only in terms of money, you are finally not seeing the world at all.

As a child, there were times when I became positively embarrassed for him in public. Haggling with shopkeepers, furious over a high price, arguing as if his very manhood were at stake. A distinct memory of how everything would wither up inside me, of wanting to be anywhere in the world except where I was. A particular incident of going with him to buy a baseball glove stands out. Every day for two weeks I had visited the store after school to admire the one I wanted. Then, when my father took me to the store one evening to buy it, he so exploded at the salesman I was afraid he was going to tear him to pieces. Frightened, sick at heart, I told him not to bother, that I didn't want the glove after all. As we were leaving the store, he offered to buy me an ice cream cone. That glove was no good anyway, he said. I'll buy you a better one some other time.

Better, of course, meant worse.

Tirades about leaving too many lights on in the house. He always made a point of buying bulbs with low wattage.

His excuse for never taking us to the movies: "Why go out and spend a fortune when it will be on television in a year or two?"

The occasional family meal in a restaurant: we always had to order the least expensive things on the menu. It became a kind of ritual. Yes, he would say, nodding his head, that's a good choice.

Years later, when my wife and I were living in New York, he would sometimes take us out to dinner. The script was always precisely the same: the moment after we had put the last forkful of food into our mouths, he would ask, "Are you ready to go?" Impossible even to consider dessert.

His utter discomfort in his own skin. His inability to sit still, to make small talk, to "relax."

It made you nervous to be with him. You felt he was always on the verge of leaving.

He loved clever little tricks, prided himself on his ability to outsmart the world at its own game. A niggardliness in the most trivial aspects of life, as ridiculous as it was depressing. With his cars, he would always disconnect the odometers, falsifying the mileage in order to guarantee himself a better trade-in price. In his house, he would always do his own repair work instead of hiring a professional. Because he had a gift for machines and knew how things worked, he would take bizarre shortcuts, using whatever materials were at hand to rig up Rube Goldberg solutions to mechanical and electrical problems—rather than spending the money to do it right.

Permanent solutions never interested him. He went on patching and patching, a little piece here, a little piece there, never allowing his boat to sink, but never giving it a chance to float either.

The way he dressed: as if twenty years behind the times. Cheap synthetic suits from the racks of discount stores; unboxed pairs of shoes from the bins of bargain basements. Beyond giving proof of his miserliness, this disregard of fashion reinforced the image of him as a man not quite in the world. The clothes he wore seemed to be an expression of solitude, a concrete way of affirming his absence. Even though he was well off, able to afford anything he wanted, he looked like a poor man, a hayseed who had just stepped off the farm.

In the last years of his life, this changed a little bit. Becoming a bachelor again had probably given him a jolt: he realized that he would have to make himself presentable if he wanted to have any kind of social life. It was not that he went out and bought expensive clothes, but at least the tone of his wardrobe changed: the dull browns and grays were abandoned for brighter colors; the outmoded style gave way to a flashier, more dapper image. Checkered pants, white shoes, yellow turtlenecks, boots with big buckles. But in spite of these efforts, he never looked quite at home in these costumes. They were not an integral part of his personality. It made you think of a little boy who had been dressed up by his parents.

Given his curious relationship to money (his desire for wealth, his inability to spend), it was somehow appropriate that he made his living among the poor. Compared to them, he was a man of enormous riches. And yet, by spending his days among people who had next to nothing, he could keep before his eyes a vision of the thing he most feared in the world: to be without money. It put things in perspective for him. He did not consider himself stingy—but sensible, a man who knew the value of a dollar. He had to be vigilant. It was the only thing that stood between him and the nightmare of poverty.

When the business was at its peak, he and his brothers owned nearly a hundred buildings. Their terrain was the grim industrial region of northern New Jersey—Jersey City, Newark—and nearly all their tenants were black. One says "slumlord," but in this case it would not have been an accurate or fair description. Nor was he in any way an absentee landlord. He was *there*, and he put in hours that would have driven even the most conscientious employee to go out on strike.

The job was a permanent juggling act. There was the buying and selling of buildings, the buying and repairing of fixtures, the managing of several teams of repair men, the renting of apartments, the supervision of the superintendents, listening to tenant complaints, dealing with the visits of building inspectors, constant involvement with the water and electric companies, not to speak of frequent visits to court—both as plaintiff and defendant—to sue for back rent, to answer to violations. Everything was always happening at once, a perpetual assault from a dozen directions at the same time, and only a man who took things in his stride could have handled it. On any given day it was impossible to do everything that had to be done. You did not go home because you were finished, but simply because it was late and you had run out of time. The next day all the problems would be waiting for you—and several new ones as well. It never stopped. In fifteen years he took only two vacations.

He was soft-hearted with the tenants—granting them delays in paying their rent, giving clothes to their children, helping them to find work—and they trusted him. Old men, afraid of being robbed, would give him their most valuable possessions to store in his office safe. Of all the brothers, he was the one people went to with their troubles. No one called him Mr. Auster. He was always Mr. Sam.

While cleaning out the house after his death, I came across this letter at the bottom of a kitchen drawer. Of all the things I found, I am happiest to have retrieved this. It somehow balances the ledger, provides me with living proof whenever my mind begins to stray too far from the facts. The letter is addressed to "Mr. Sam," and the handwriting is nearly illegible.

April 19, 1976

Dear Sam,

I know you are so surprised to hear from me. first of all maybe I better introduce my self to you. I'm Mrs. Nash. I'm Albert Groover Sister in law—Mrs. Groover and Albert that lived at 285 pine Street in Jersey City so long and Mrs. Banks thats my Sister too. Any way. if you can remember.

You made arrangement to get the apartment for my children and I at 327 Johnston Ave right around the Corner from Mr. & Mrs. Groover my Sister.

Anyway I move away left of owing a $40. rent. this was the year of 1964 but I didn't for get I owed this earnest debt. So now here is your money. thanks for being so very nice to the children and I at that time. this is how much I appreciated what you done for us. I hope you can recall back to the time. So you was never forgotten by me.

About 3 weeks ago I called the office but weren't in at that time. may the Good Lord ever to Bless you. I hardly comes to Jersey City if so I would stop by see you.

No matter now I am happy to pay this debt. All for now.

Sincerely

   Mrs. JB. Nash

As a boy, I would occasionally go the rounds with him as he collected rent. I was too young to understand what I was seeing, but I remember the impression it made on me, as if, precisely because I did not understand, the raw perceptions of these experiences went directly into me, where they remain today; as immediate as a splinter in the thumb.

The wooden buildings with their dark, inhospitable hallways. And behind each door, a horde of children playing in a bare apartment; a mother, always sullen, overworked, tired, bent over an ironing board. Most vivid is the smell, as if poverty were more than a lack of money, but a physical sensation, a stench that invaded your head and made it impossible to think. Every time I walked into a building with my father, I would hold my breath, not daring to breathe, as if that smell were going to hurt me. Everyone was always happy to meet Mr. Sam's son. I was given innumerable smiles and pats on the head.

Once, when I was a bit older, I can remember driving with him down a street in Jersey City and seeing a boy wearing a T-shirt I had outgrown several months before. It was a very distinctive shirt, with a peculiar combination of yellow and blue stripes, and there was no question that this was the one that had been mine. Unaccountably, I was overcome with a feeling of shame.

Older still, at thirteen, fourteen, fifteen, I would sometimes go in with him to earn money working with the carpenters, painters, and repair men. Once, on an excruciatingly hot day in the middle of summer, I was given the job of helping one of the men tar a roof. The man's name was Joe Levine (a black man who had changed his name to Levine out of gratitude to an old Jewish grocer who had helped him in his youth), and he was my father's most trusted and reliable handyman. We hauled several fifty gallon barrels of tar up to the roof and got to work spreading the stuff over the surface with brooms. The sunlight beating down on that flat black roof was brutal, and after half an hour or so I became extremely dizzy, slipped on a patch of wet tar, fell, and somehow knocked over one of the open barrels, which then spilled tar all over me.

When I got back to the office a few minutes later, my father was greatly amused. I realized that the situation was amusing, but I was too embarrassed to want to joke about it. To my father's credit, he did not get angry at me or make fun of me. He laughed, but in a way that made me laugh too. Then he dropped what he had been doing, took me to the Woolworth's across the street, and bought me some new clothes. It had suddenly become possible for me to feel close to him.

As the years went by, the business started to decline. The business itself was not at fault, but rather the nature of the business: at that particular time, in that particular place, it was no longer possible to survive. The cities were falling apart, and no one seemed to care. What had once been a more or less fulfilling

activity for my father now became simple drudgery. In the last
years of his life he hated going to work.

Vandalism became such a severe problem that doing any kind
of repairs became a demoralizing gesture. No sooner was plumb-
ing installed in a building than the pipes would be ripped out by
thieves. Windows were constantly being broken, doors smashed,
hallways gutted, fires started. At the same time, it was impossible
to sell out. No one wanted the buildings. The only way to get rid
of them was to abandon them and let the cities take over. Tremen-
dous amounts of money were lost in this way, an entire life's
work. In the end, at the time of my father's death, there were only
six or seven buildings left. The whole empire had disintegrated.

The last time I was in Jersey City (at least ten years ago) the
place had the look of a disaster area, as if it had been pillaged
by Huns. Gray, desolate streets; garbage piled everywhere; dere-
licts shuffling aimlessly up and down. My father's office had
been robbed so many times that by now there was nothing left
in it but some gray metal desks, a few chairs, and three or four
telephones. Not even a typewriter, not one touch of color. It
was not really a work place anymore, but a room in hell. I sat
down and looked out at the bank across the street. No one
came out, no one went in. The only living things were two stray
dogs humping on the steps.

How he managed to pick himself up and go in there every
day is beyond my understanding. Force of habit, or else sheer
stubbornness. Not only was it depressing, it was dangerous. He
was mugged several times, and once was kicked in the head so
viciously by an attacker that his hearing was permanently dam-
aged. For the last four or five years of his life there was a faint
and constant ringing in his head, a humming that never went
away, not even while he was asleep. The doctors said there was
nothing that could be done about it.

In the end, he never went out into the street without carrying
a monkey wrench in his right hand. He was over sixty-five years
old, and he did not want to take any more chances.

Two sentences that suddenly come to mind this morning as I
am showing Daniel how to make scrambled eggs.

" 'And now I want to know,' the woman says, with terrible force, 'I want to know whether it is possible to find another father like him anywhere in the world.' " (Isaac Babel)

"Children have always a tendency either to depreciate or to exalt their parents, and to a good son his father is always the best of fathers, quite apart from any objective reason there may be for admiring him." (Proust)

I realize now that I must have been a bad son. Or, if not precisely bad, then at least a disappointment, a source of confusion and sadness. It made no sense to him that he had produced a poet for a son. Nor could he understand why a young man with two degrees from Columbia University should take a job after graduation as an ordinary seaman on an oil tanker in the Gulf of Mexico, and then, without rhyme or reason, take off for Paris and spend four years there leading a hand to mouth existence.

His most common description of me was that I had "my head in the clouds," or else that I "did not have my feet on the ground." Either way, I must not have seemed very substantial to him, as if I were somehow a vapor or a person not wholly of this world. In his eyes, you became part of the world by working. By definition, work was something that brought in money. If it did not bring in money, it was not work. Writing, therefore, was not work, especially the writing of poetry. At best it was a hobby, a pleasant way to pass the time in between the things that really mattered. My father thought that I was squandering my gifts, refusing to grow up.

Nevertheless, some kind of bond remained between us. We were not close, but stayed in touch. A phone call every month or so, perhaps three or four visits a year. Each time a book of my poetry was published I would dutifully send it to him, and he would always call to thank me. Whenever I wrote an article for a magazine, I would set aside a copy and make sure I gave it to him the next time I saw him. *The New York Review of Books* meant nothing to him, but the pieces in *Commentary* impressed him. I think he felt that if the Jews were publishing me, then perhaps there was something to it.

Once, while I was still living in Paris, he wrote to tell me he had gone to the public library to read some of my poems that had appeared in a recent issue of *Poetry*. I imagined him in a large, deserted room, early in the morning before going to work: sitting at one of those long tables with his overcoat still on, hunched over words that must have been incomprehensible to him.

I have tried to keep this image in mind, along with all the others that will not leave it.

The rampant, totally mystifying force of contradiction. I understand now that each fact is nullified by the next fact, that each thought engenders an equal and opposite thought. Impossible to say anything without reservation: he was good, or he was bad; he was this, or he was that. All of them are true. At times I have the feeling that I am writing about three or four different men, each one distinct, each one a contradiction of all the others. Fragments. Or the anecdote as a form of knowledge.

Yes.

The occasional flash of generosity. At those rare times when the world was not a threat to him, his motive for living seemed to be kindness. "May the good Lord ever to Bless you."

Friends called him whenever they were in trouble. A car stuck somewhere in the middle of the night, and my father would drag himself out of bed and come to the rescue. In certain ways it was easy for others to take advantage of him. He refused to complain about anything.

A patience that bordered on the superhuman. He was the only person I have ever known who could teach someone to drive without getting angry or crumpling in a fit of nerves. You could be careening straight toward a lamp post, and still he would not get excited.

Impenetrable. And because of that, at times almost serene.

Starting when he was still a young man, he always took a special interest in his oldest nephew—the only child of his only sister. My aunt had an unhappy life, punctuated by a series of difficult marriages, and her son bore the brunt of it: shipped off to military schools, never really given a home. Motivated, I think, by nothing more than kindness and a sense of duty, my father took the boy under his wing. He nursed him along with constant encouragement, taught him how to get along in the world. Later, he helped him in business, and whenever a problem came up, he was always ready to listen and give advice. Even after my cousin married and had his own family, my father continued to take an active interest, putting them up in his house at one point for more than a year, religiously giving presents to his four grand-nephews and grand-nieces on their birthdays, and often going to visit them for dinner.

This cousin was more shaken by my father's death than any of my other relatives. At the family gathering after the funeral he came up to me three or four times and said, "I ran into him by accident just the other day. We were supposed to have dinner together Friday night."

The words he used were exactly the same each time. As if he no longer knew what he was saying.

I felt that we had somehow reversed roles, that he was the grieving son and I was the sympathetic nephew. I wanted to put my arm around his shoulder and tell him what a good man his father had been. After all, he was the real son, he was the son I could never bring myself to be.

For the past two weeks, these lines from Maurice Blanchot echoing in my head: "One thing must be understood: I have said nothing extraordinary or even surprising. What is extraordinary begins at the moment I stop. But I am no longer able to speak of it."

To begin with death. To work my way back into life, and then, finally, to return to death.

Or else: the vanity of trying to say anything about anyone.

In 1972 he came to visit me in Paris. It was the one time he ever traveled to Europe.

I was living that year in a minuscule sixth-floor maid's room barely large enough for a bed, a table, a chair, and a sink. The windows and little balcony stared into the face of one of the stone angels that jutted from St. Germain Auxerrois: the Louvre to my left, Les Halles off to my right, and Montmartre in the far distance ahead. I had a great fondness for that room, and many of the poems that later appeared in my first book were written there.

My father was not planning to stay for any length of time, hardly even what you would call a vacation: four days in London, three days in Paris, and then home again. But I was pleased at the thought of seeing him and prepared myself to show him a good time.

Two things happened, however, that made this impossible. I became very ill with the flu; and I had to leave for Mexico the day after his arrival to work on a ghostwriting project.

I waited for him all morning in the lobby of the tourist hotel where he had booked reservations, sweating away with a high fever, almost delirious with weakness. When he did not show up at the appointed time, I stayed on for another hour or two, but finally gave in and went back to my room where I collapsed into bed.

Late in the afternoon he came and knocked on my door, waking me from a deep sleep. The encounter was straight out of Dostoyevsky: bourgeois father comes to visit son in a foreign city and finds the struggling poet alone in a garret, wasting away with fever. He was shocked by what he saw, outraged that anyone could live in such a room, and it galvanized him into action: he made me put on my coat, dragged me off to a neighborhood clinic, and then bought the pills that were prescribed for me. Afterwards, he refused to allow me to spend the night in my room. I was in no condition to argue, so I agreed to stay in his hotel.

The next day I was no better. But there were things to be done, and I picked myself up and did them. In the morning I took my father along with me to the vast Avenue Henri Martin apartment of the movie producer who was sending me to Mexico. For the past year I had been working on and off for this man, doing what amounted to odd jobs—translations, script synopses—things that were only marginally connected to the movies, which anyway did not interest me. Each project was more idiotic than the last, but the pay was good, and I needed the money. Now he wanted me to help his Mexican wife with a book she had been contracted to write for an English publisher: Quetzalcoatl and the mysteries of the plumed serpent. This seemed to be pushing it a bit, and I had already turned him down several times. But each time I said no, his offer had gone up, until now I was being paid so much money that I could no longer turn away. I would only be gone for a month, and I was being paid in cash—in advance.

This was the transaction my father witnessed. For once, I could see that he was impressed. Not only had I led him into this luxurious setting and introduced him to a man who did business in the millions, but now this man was calmly handing me a stack of hundred dollar bills across the table and telling me to have a pleasant trip. It was the money, of course, that made the difference, the fact that my father had seen it with his own eyes. I felt it as a triumph, as if I had somehow been vindicated. For the first time he had been forced to realize that I could take care of myself on my own terms.

He became very protective, indulgent of my weakened condition. Helped me deposit the money in the bank, all smiles and jokes. Then got us a cab and rode all the way to the airport with me. A big handshake at the end. Good luck, son. Knock 'em dead.

You bet.

Nothing now for several days. . . .

In spite of the excuses I have made for myself, I understand what is happening. The closer I come to the end of what I am able to say, the more reluctant I am to say anything. I want to postpone the moment of ending, and in this way delude myself into thinking that I have only just begun, that the better part of my story still lies ahead. No matter how useless these words might seem to be, they have nevertheless stood between me and a silence that continues to terrify me. When I step into this silence, it will mean that my father has vanished forever.

The dingy green carpet in the funeral home. And the director, unctuous, professional, suffering from eczema and swollen ankles, going down a checklist of expenses as if I were about to buy a suite of bedroom furniture on credit. He handed me an envelope that contained the ring my father had been wearing when he died. Idly fingering the ring as the conversation droned on, I noticed that the underside of the stone was smeared with the residue of some soapy lubricant. A few moments passed before I made the connection, and then it became absurdly obvious: the lotion had been used to remove the ring from his finger. I tried to imagine the person whose job it was to do such things. I did not feel horror so much as fascination. I remember thinking to myself: I have entered the world of facts, the realm of brute particulars. The ring was gold, with a black setting that bore the insignia of the Masonic brotherhood. My father had not been an active member for over twenty years.

The funeral director kept telling me how he had known my father "in the old days," implying an intimacy and friendship I was sure had never existed. As I gave him the information to be passed on to the newspapers for the obituary, he anticipated my remarks with incorrect facts, rushing ahead of me in order to prove how well acquainted he had been with my father. Each time this happened, I stopped and corrected him. The next day, when the obituary appeared in the paper, many of these incorrect facts were printed.

Three days before he died, my father had bought a new car. He had driven it once, maybe twice, and when I returned to his house after the funeral, I saw it sitting in the garage, already defunct, like some huge, stillborn creature. Later that same day I went off to the garage for a moment to be by myself. I sat down behind the wheel of this car, inhaling the strange factory newness of it. The odometer read sixty-seven miles. That also happened to have been my father's age: sixty-seven years. The brevity of it sickened me. As if that were the distance between life and death. A tiny trip, hardly longer than a drive to the next town.

Worst regret: that I was not given a chance to see him after he died. Ignorantly, I had assumed the coffin would be open during the funeral service, and then, when it wasn't, it was too late to do anything about it.

Never to have seen him dead deprives me of an anguish I would have welcomed. It is not that his death has been made any less real, but now, each time I want to see it, each time I want to touch its reality, I must engage in an act of imagination. There is nothing to remember. Nothing but a kind of emptiness.

When the grave was uncovered to receive the coffin, I noticed a thick orange root thrusting into the hole. It had a strangely calming effect on me. For a brief moment the bare fact of death could no longer be hidden behind the words and gestures of ceremony. Here it was: unmediated, unadorned, impossible to turn my eyes away from. My father was being lowered into the ground, and in time, as the coffin gradually disintegrated, his body would help to feed the same root I had seen. More than anything that had been said or done that day, this made sense to me.

The rabbi who conducted the funeral service was the same man who had presided over my Bar Mitzvah nineteen years earlier. The last time I had seen him he was a youngish, clean-shaven man. Now he was old, with a full gray beard. He had not known my father, in fact knew nothing about him, and half an hour before the service was to begin I sat down with him and told him what to say in the eulogy. He made notes on little scraps of paper. When it came time for him to deliver the speech, he spoke with great feeling. The subject was a man he had never known, and yet he made it sound as though he were speaking from the heart. Behind me, I could hear women sobbing. He was following what I had told him almost word for word.

It occurs to me that I began writing this story a long time ago, long before my father died.

Night after night, lying awake in bed, my eyes open in the darkness. The impossibility of sleep, the impossibility of not thinking about how he died. I find myself sweating between the sheets, trying to imagine what it feels like to suffer a heart attack.

Adrenalin pumps through me, my head pounds, and my whole
body seems to contract into a small area behind my chest. A
need to experience the same panic, the same mortal pain.

And then, at night, there are the dreams, nearly every night.
In one of them, which woke me up just hours ago, I learned
from the teenage daughter of my father's lady friend that she,
the daughter, had been made pregnant by my father. Because
she was so young, it was agreed that my wife and I would raise
the child after it was born. The baby was going to be a boy.
Everyone knew this in advance.

It is equally true, perhaps, that once this story has ended, it
will go on telling itself, even after the words have been used up.

The old gentleman at the funeral was my great-uncle, Sam
Auster, now almost ninety years old. Tall, hairless, a high-
pitched, rasping voice. Not a word about the events of 1919,
and I did not have the heart to ask him. I took care of Sam
when he was a little boy, he said. But that was all.

When asked if he wanted anything to drink, he requested a
glass of hot water. Lemon? No thank you, just hot water.

Again Blanchot: "But I am no longer able to speak of it."

From the house: a document from St. Clair County in the State
of Alabama duly announcing my parents' divorce. The signature at the bottom: Ann W. Love.

From the house: a watch, a few sweaters, a jacket, an alarm
clock, six tennis rackets, and an old rusted Buick that barely
runs. A set of dishes, a coffee table, three or four lamps. A bar-
room statue of Johnnie Walker for Daniel. The blank photograph album, This Is Our Life: The Austers.

At first I thought it would be a comfort to hold on to these
things, that they would remind me of my father and make me
think of him as I went about my life. But objects, it seems, are
no more than objects. I am used to them now, I have begun to
think of them as my own. I read time by his watch, I wear his
sweaters, I drive around in his car. But all this is no more than
an illusion of intimacy. I have already appropriated these

things. My father has vanished from them, has become invisible again. And sooner or later they will break down, fall apart, and have to be thrown away. I doubt that it will even seem to matter.

". . . here it holds good that only he who works gets the bread, only he who was in anguish finds repose, only he who descends into the underworld rescues the beloved, only he who draws the knife gets Isaac. . . . He who will not work must take note of what is written about the maidens of Israel, for he gives birth to the wind, but he who is willing to work gives birth to his own father." (Kierkegaard)

Past two in the morning. An overflowing ashtray, an empty coffee cup, and the cold of early spring. An image of Daniel now, as he lies upstairs in his crib asleep. To end with this.

To wonder what he will make of these pages when he is old enough to read them.

And the image of his sweet and ferocious little body, as he lies upstairs in his crib asleep. To end with this.

(1979)

THE BOOK OF MEMORY

"When the dead weep, they are beginning to recover," said the Crow solemnly.

"I am sorry to contradict my famous friend and colleague," said the Owl, "but as far as I'm concerned, I think that when the dead weep, it means they do not want to die."

—Collodi, *The Adventures of Pinocchio*

He lays out a piece of blank paper on the table before him and writes these words with his pen. It was. It will never be again.

Later that same day he returns to his room. He finds a fresh sheet of paper and lays it out on the table before him. He writes until he has covered the entire page with words. Later, when he reads over what he has written, he has trouble deciphering the words. Those he does manage to understand do not seem to say what he thought he was saying. Then he goes out to eat his dinner.

That night he tells himself that tomorow is another day. New words begin to clamor in his head, but he does not write them down. He decides to refer to himself as A. He walks back and forth between the table and the window. He turns on the radio and then turns it off. He smokes a cigarette.

Then he writes. It was. It will never be again.

Christmas Eve, 1979. His life no longer seemed to dwell in the present. Whenever he turned on his radio and listened to the news of the world, he would find himself imagining the words to be describing things that had happened long ago. Even as he stood in the present, he felt himself to be looking at it from the future, and this present-as-past was so antiquated that even the horrors of the day, which ordinarily would have filled him with outrage, seemed remote to him, as if the voice in the radio were reading from a chronicle of some lost civilization.

Later, in a time of greater clarity, he would refer to this sensa-tion as "nostalgia for the present."

To follow with a detailed description of classical memory systems, complete with charts, diagrams, symbolic drawings. Raymond Lull, for example, or Robert Fludd, not to speak of Giordano Bruno, the great Nolan burned at the stake in 1600. Places and images as catalysts for remembering other places and images: things, events, the buried artifacts of one's own life. Mnemotechnics. To follow with Bruno's notion that the structure of human thought corresponds to the structure of na-ture. And therefore to conclude that everything, in some sense, is connected to everything else.

At the same time, as if running parallel to the above, a brief dis-quisition on the room. An image, for example, of a man sitting alone in a room. As in Pascal: "All the unhappiness of man stems from one thing only: that he is incapable of staying qui-etly in his room." As in the phrase: "he wrote The Book of Memory in this room."

The Book of Memory. Book One.

Christmas Eve, 1979. He is in New York, alone in his little room at 6 Varick Street. Like many of the buildings in the neigh-borhood, this one used to be nothing but a work place. Rem-nants of its former life are everywhere around him: networks of mysterious pipes, sooty tin ceilings, hissing steam radiators. Whenever his eyes fall on the frosted glass panel of his door, he can read these clumsily stencilled letters in reverse: R.M. Pooley, Licensed Electrician. People were never supposed to live here. It is a room meant for machines, cuspidors, and sweat.

He cannot call it home, but for the past nine months it is all he has had. A few dozen books, a mattress on the floor, a table, three chairs, a hot plate, and a corroded cold water sink. The toilet is down the hall, but he uses it only when he has to shit. Pissing he does in the sink. For the past three days the elevator has been out of service, and since this is the top floor, it has made him reluctant to go out. It is not so much that he dreads climbing the ten flights of stairs when he gets back, but that he finds it disheartening to exhaust himself so thoroughly only to return to such bleakness. By staying in this room for long stretches at a time, he can usually manage to fill it with his thoughts, and this in turn seems to dispel the dreariness, or at least make him unaware of it. Each time he goes out, he takes his thoughts with him, and during his absence the room gradually empties of his efforts to inhabit it. When he returns, he has to begin the process all over again, and that takes work, real spiritual work. Considering his physical condition after the climb (chest heaving like a bellows, legs as tight and heavy as tree trunks), this inner struggle takes all that much longer to get started. In the interim, in the void between the moment he opens the door and the moment he begins to reconquer the emptiness, his mind flails in a wordless panic. It is as if he were being forced to watch his own disappearance, as if, by crossing the threshold of this room, he were entering another dimension, taking up residence inside a black hole.

Above him, dim clouds float past the tar-stained skylight, drifting off into the Manhattan evening. Below him, he hears the traffic rushing toward the Holland Tunnel: streams of cars heading home to New Jersey on the night before Christmas. Next door it is quiet. The Pomponio brothers, who arrive there each morning to smoke their cigars and grind out plastic display letters—a business they keep going by working twelve or fourteen hours a day—are probably at home, getting ready to eat a holiday meal. That is all to the good. Lately, one of them has been spending the night in his shop, and his snoring invariably keeps A. awake. The man sleeps directly opposite A., on the other side of the thin wall that divides their two rooms, and hour after hour A. lies in bed, staring into the darkness, trying to pace his thoughts to the ebb and flow of the man's troubled, adenoidal dreams. The snores swell gradually, and at the peak of each cycle they become long, piercing, almost hysterical, as if, when night comes, the snorer had to imitate the noise of the machine that holds him captive during the day. For once A. can count on a calm, unbroken sleep. Not even the arrival of Santa Claus will disturb him.

Winter solstice: the darkest time of the year. No sooner has he woken up in the morning than he feels the day beginning to slip away from him. There is no light to sink his teeth into, no sense of time unfolding. Rather, a feeling of doors being shut, of locks being turned. It is a hermetic season, a long moment of inwardness. The outer world, the tangible world of materials and bodies, has come to seem no more than an emanation of his mind. He feels himself sliding through events, hovering like a ghost around his own presence, as if he were living somewhere to the side of himself—not really here, but not anywhere else either. A feeling of having been locked up, and at the same time of being able to walk through walls. He notes somewhere in the margins of a thought: a darkness in the bones; make a note of this.

By day, heat gushes from the radiators at full blast. Even now, in coldest winter, he is forced to keep the window open. At night, however, there is no heat at all. He sleeps fully clothed, with two or three sweaters, curled up tightly in a sleeping bag. During the weekends, the heat is off altogether, both day and night, and there have been times lately when he has sat at his table, trying to write, and could not feel the pen in his hand anymore. In itself, this lack of comfort does not disturb him. But it has the effect of keeping him off balance, of prodding him into a state of constant inner watchfulness. In spite of what it might seem to be, this room is not a retreat from the world. There is nothing here to welcome him, no promise of a soma holiday to woo him into oblivion. These four walls hold only the signs of his own disquiet, and in order to find some measure of peace in these surroundings, he must dig more and more deeply into himself. But the more he digs, the less there will be to go on digging into. This seems undeniable to him. Sooner or later, he is bound to use himself up.

When night comes, the electricity dims to half-strength, then goes up again, then comes down, for no apparent reason. It is as though the lights were controlled by some prankster deity. Con Edison has no record of the place, and no one has ever had to pay for power. At the same time, the phone company has refused to acknowledge A.'s existence. The phone has been here for nine months, functioning without a flaw, but he had not yet received a bill for it. When he called the other day to straighten out the problem, they insisted they had never heard of him.

Somehow, he has managed to escape the clutches of the computer, and none of his calls has ever been recorded. His name is off the books. If he felt like it, he could spend his idle moments making free calls to faraway places. But the fact is, there is no one he wants to talk to. Not in California, not in Paris, not in China. The world has shrunk to the size of this room for him, and for as long as it takes him to understand it, he must stay where he is. Only one thing is certain: he cannot be anywhere until he is here. And if he does not manage to find this place, it would be absurd for him to think of looking for another.

Life inside the whale. A gloss on Jonah, and what it means to refuse to speak. Parallel text: Gepetto in the belly of the shark (whale in the Disney version), and the story of how Pinocchio rescues him. Is it true that one must dive to the depths of the sea and save one's father to become a real boy?

Initial statement of these themes. Further installments to follow.

Then shipwreck. Crusoe on his island. "That boy might be happy if he would stay at home, but if he goes abroad he will be the most miserable wretch that was ever born." Solitary consciousness. Or in George Oppen's phrase: "the shipwreck of the singular."

A vision of waves all around, water as endless as air, and the jungle heat behind. "I am divided from mankind, a solitaire, one banished from human society."

And Friday? No, not yet. There is no Friday, at least not here. Everything that happens is prior to that moment. Or else: the waves will have washed the footprints away.

First commentary on the nature of chance.

This is where it begins. A friend of his tells him a story. Several years go by, and then he finds himself thinking about the story again. It is not that it begins with the story. Rather, in the act of remembering it, he has become aware that something is happening to him. For the story would not have occurred to him unless whatever summoned its memory had not already been making itself felt. Unknown to himself, he had been burrowing down to a place of almost vanished memory, and now that something had surfaced, he could not even guess how long the excavation had taken.

During the war, M.'s father had hidden out from the Nazis for several months in a Paris *chambre de bonne*. Eventually, he managed to escape, made his way to America, and began a new life. Years passed, more than twenty years. M. had been born, had grown up, and was now going off to study in Paris. Once there, he spent several difficult weeks looking for a place to live. Just when he was about to give up in despair, he found a small *chambre de bonne*. Immediately upon moving in, he wrote a letter to his father to tell him the good news. A week or so later he received a reply: your address, wrote M.'s father, that is the same building I hid out in during the war. He then went on to describe the details of the room. It turned out to be the same room his son had rented.

It begins, therefore, with this room. And then it begins with that room. And beyond that there is the father, there is the son, and there is the war. To speak of fear, and to remember that the man who hid in that little room was a Jew. To note as well: that the city was Paris, a place A. had just returned from (December fifteenth), and that for a whole year he once lived in a Paris *chambre de bonne*—where he wrote his first book of poems, and where his own father, on his only trip to Europe, once came to see him. To remember his father's death. And beyond that, to understand— this most important of all—that M.'s story has no meaning.

Nevertheless, this is where it begins. The first word appears only at a moment when nothing can be explained anymore, at some instant of experience that defies all sense. To be reduced to saying nothing. Or else, to say to himself: this is what haunts me. And then to realize, almost in the same breath, that this is what he haunts.

He lays out a blank sheet of paper on the table before him and writes these words with his pen. Possible epigraph for The Book of Memory.

Then he opens a book by Wallace Stevens *(Opus Posthumous)* and copies out the following sentence.

"In the presence of extraordinary reality, consciousness takes the place of imagination."

Later that same day he writes steadily for three or four hours. Afterwards, when he reads over what he has written, he finds only one paragraph of any interest. Although he is not sure what to make of it, he decides to keep it for future reference and copies it into a lined notebook:

When the father dies, he writes, the son becomes his own father and his own son. He looks at his son and sees himself in the face of the boy. He imagines what the boy sees when he looks at him and finds himself becoming his own father. Inexplicably, he is moved by this. It is not just the sight of the boy that moves him, nor even the thought of standing inside his father, but what he sees in the boy of his own vanished past. It is a nostalgia for his own life that he feels, perhaps, a memory of his own boyhood as a son to his father. Inexplicably, he finds himself shaking at that moment with both happiness and sorrow, if this is possible, as if he were going both forward and backward, into the future and into the past. And there are times, often there are times, when these feelings are so strong that his life no longer seems to dwell in the present.

Memory as a place, as a building, as a sequence of columns, cornices, porticoes. The body inside the mind, as if we were moving around in there, going from one place to the next, and the sound of our footsteps as we walk, moving from one place to the next.

"One must consequently employ a large number of places," writes Cicero, "which must be well lighted, clearly set out in order, spaced out at moderate intervals; and images which are active, sharply defined, unusual, and which have the power of speedily encountering and penetrating the psyche. . . . For the places are very much like wax tablets or papyrus, the images like the letters, the arrangement and disposition of the images like the script, and the speaking like the reading."

He returned from Paris ten days ago. He had gone there on a work visit, and it was the first time he had been abroad in more

than five years. The business of traveling, of continual conversation, of too much drinking with old friends, of being away
from his little son for so long, had finally worn him out. With a
few days to spare at the end of his trip, he decided to go to Amsterdam, a city he had never been to before. He thought: the
paintings. But once there, it was a thing he had not planned on
doing that made the greatest impression on him. For no particular reason (idly looking through a guide book he found in his
hotel room) he decided to go to Anne Frank's house, which has
been preserved as a museum. It was a Sunday morning, gray
with rain, and the streets along the canal were deserted. He
climbed the steep and narrow staircase inside the house and entered the secret annex. As he stood in Anne Frank's room, the
room in which the diary was written, now bare, with the faded
pictures of Hollywood movie stars she had collected still pasted
to the walls, he suddenly found himself crying. Not sobbing, as
might happen in response to a deep inner pain, but crying without sound, the tears streaming down his cheeks, as if purely in
response to the world. It was at that moment, he later realized,
that The Book of Memory began. As in the phrase: "she wrote
her diary in this room."

From the window of that room, facing out on the backyard,
you can see the rear windows of a house in which Descartes
once lived. There are children's swings in the yard now, toys
scattered in the grass, pretty little flowers. As he looked out the
window that day, he wondered if the children those toys belonged to had any idea of what had happened thirty-five years
earlier in the spot where he was standing. And if they did, what
it would be like to grow up in the shadow of Anne Frank's
room.

To repeat Pascal: "All the unhappiness of man stems from
one thing only: that he is incapable of staying quietly in his
room." At roughly the same time these words entered the *Pensées*, Descartes wrote to a friend in France from his room in
that house in Amsterdam. "Is there any country," he asked with
exuberance, "in which one can enjoy freedom as enormously as
one does here?" Everything, in some sense, can be read as a
gloss on everything else. To imagine Anne Frank, for example,

had she lived on after the war, reading Descartes' *Meditations* as a university student in Amsterdam. To imagine a solitude so crushing, so unconsolable, that one stops breathing for hundreds of years.

He notes, with a certain fascination, that Anne Frank's birthday is the same as his son's. June twelfth. Under the sign of Gemini. An image of the twins. A world in which everything is double, in which the same thing always happens twice.

Memory: the space in which a thing happens for the second time.

The Book of Memory. Book Two.

Israel Lichtenstein's Last Testament. Warsaw; July 31, 1942.

"With zeal and zest I threw myself into the work to help assemble archive materials. I was entrusted to be the custodian. I hid the material. Besides me, no one knew. I confided only in my friend Hersh Wasser, my supervisor. . . . It is well hidden. Please God that it be preserved. That will be the finest and best we achieved in the present gruesome time. . . . I know that we will not endure. To survive and remain alive after such horrible murders and massacres is impossible. Therefore I write this testament of mine. Perhaps I am not worthy of being remembered, but just for my grit in working with the Society Oneg Shabbat and for being the most endangered because I hid the entire material. It would be a small thing to give my own head. I risk the head of my dear wife Gele Seckstein and my treasure, my little daughter, Margalit. . . . I don't want any gratitude, any monument, any praise. I want only a remembrance, so that my family, brother and sister abroad, may know what has become of my remains. . . . I want my wife to be remembered. Gele Seckstein, artist, dozens of works, talented, didn't manage to exhibit, did not show in public. During the three years of war worked among children as educator, teacher, made stage sets, costumes for the children's productions, received awards. Now together with me, we are preparing to receive death. . . . I want my little daughter to be remembered. Margalit, 20 months old today. Has mastered Yiddish perfectly, speaks a pure Yiddish.

At 9 months began to speak Yiddish clearly. In intelligence she is on a par with 3- or 4-year old children. I don't want to brag about her. Witnesses to this, who tell me about it, are the teaching staff of the school at Nowolipki 68. . . . I am not sorry about my life and that of my wife. But I am sorry for the gifted little girl. She deserves to be remembered also. . . . May we be the redeemers for all the rest of the Jews in the whole world. I believe in the survival of our people. Jews will not be annihilated. We, the Jews of Poland, Czechoslovakia, Lithuania, Latvia, are the scapegoat for all Israel in all the other lands."

Standing and watching. Sitting down. Lying in bed. Walking through the streets. Eating his meals at the Square Diner, alone in a booth, a newspaper spread out on the table before him. Opening his mail. Writing letters. Standing and watching. Walking through the streets. Learning from an old English friend, T., that both their families had originally come from the same town (Stanislav) in Eastern Europe. Before World War I it had been part of the Austro-Hungarian Empire; between the wars it had been part of Poland; and now, since the end of World War II, part of the Soviet Union. In the first letter from T. there is some speculation that they might, after all, be cousins. A second letter, however, offers clarification. T. has learned from an ancient aunt that in Stanislav his family was quite wealthy; A.'s family, on the other hand (and this is consistent with everything he has ever known), was poor. The story is that one of A.'s relatives (an uncle or cousin of some sort) lived in a small cottage on the property of T.'s family. He fell in love with the young lady of the household, proposed marriage, and was turned down. At that point he left Stanislav forever.

What A. finds particularly fascinating about this story is that the man's name was precisely the same as his son's.

Some weeks later he reads the following entry in the Jewish Encyclopedia:

AUSTER, DANIEL (1893–1962). Israel lawyer and mayor of Jerusalem. Auster, who was born in Stanislav (then Western Galicia), studied law in Vienna, graduated in 1914, and moved to Palestine. During World War I he served in the Austrian expeditionary force headquarters in Damascus, where he assisted Arthur Ruppin in sending financial help from Constantinople to the starving *yishuv*. After the war he established a law practice in Jerusalem that represented several Jewish-Arab interests, and served as secretary of the Legal Department of the Zionist Commission (1919, 20). In 1934 Auster was elected a Jerusalem councillor; in 1935 he was appointed deputy mayor of Jerusalem; and in 1936–38 and 1944–45 he was acting mayor. Auster represented the Jewish case against internationalization of Jerusalem brought before the United Nations in 1947–48. In 1948 Auster (who represented the Progressive Party) was elected mayor of Jerusalem, the first to hold that office in an independent Israel. Auster held that post until 1951. He also served as a member of the Provisional Council of Israel in 1948. He headed the Israel United Nations Association from its inception until his death."

All during the three days he spent in Amsterdam, he was lost. The plan of the city is circular (a series of concentric circles, bisected by canals, a cross-hatch of hundreds of tiny bridges, each one connecting to another, and then another, as though endlessly), and you cannot simply "follow" a street as you can in other cities. To get somewhere you have to know in advance where you are going. A. did not, since he was a stranger, and moreover found himself curiously reluctant to consult a map. For three days it rained, and for three days he walked around in circles. He realized that in comparison to New York (or New Amsterdam, as he was fond of saying to himself after he returned), Amsterdam was a small place, a city whose streets could probably be memorized in ten days. And yet, even if he was lost, would it not have been possible for him to ask directions of some passerby? Theoretically, yes, but in fact he was unable to bring himself to do so. It was not that he was afraid of strangers, nor that he was physically reluctant to speak. More subtly, he found himself hesitating to speak English to the Dutch. Nearly everyone speaks excellent English in Amsterdam. This ease of communication, however, was upsetting to him, as if it would somehow rob the place of its foreignness. Not in the sense that he was seeking the exotic, but in the sense that the place would no longer be itself—as if the Dutch, by speaking English, would be denied their Dutchness. If he could have been sure that no one would understand him, he would not have hesitated to rush up to a stranger and speak English, in a comical effort to make himself understood: with words, gestures, grimaces, etc. As it was, he felt himself unwilling to violate the Dutch people's Dutchness, even though they themselves had long ago allowed it to be violated. He therefore held his tongue. He wandered. He walked around in circles. He allowed himself to be lost. Sometimes, he later discovered, he would be only a few feet from his destination, but not knowing where to turn, would then go off in the wrong direction, thereby taking himself farther and farther from where he thought he was going. It occurred to him that perhaps he was wandering in the circles of hell, that the city had been designed as a model of the underworld, based on some classical representation of the place. Then he remembered that various diagrams of hell had been used as memory systems by some of the sixteenth century writers on the subject. (Cosmas Rossellius, for example, in his *Thesaurus Artificiosae Memoriae*, Venice, 1579). And if Amsterdam was hell, and if hell was memory, then he realized that perhaps there was some purpose to his being lost. Cut off from everything that was familiar to him, unable to discover even a single point of reference, he saw that his steps, by taking him nowhere, were taking him nowhere but into himself. He was wandering inside himself, and he was lost. Far from troubling him, this state of being lost became a source of happiness, of exhilaration. He breathed it into his very bones. As if on the brink of some previously hidden knowledge, he breathed it into his very bones and said to himself, almost triumphantly: I am lost.

His life no longer seemed to dwell in the present. Each time he saw a child, he would try to imagine what it would look like as a grown-up. Each time he saw an old person, he would try to imagine what that person had looked like as a child.

It was worst with women, especially if the woman was young and beautiful. He could not help looking through the skin of her face and imagining the anonymous skull behind it. And the more lovely the face, the more ardent his attempt to seek in it the encroaching signs of the future: the incipient wrinkles, the later-to-be-sagging chin, the glaze of disappointment in the eyes. He would put one face on top of another: this woman at forty; this woman at sixty; this woman at eighty; as if, even as he stood in the present, he felt compelled to hunt out the future, to track down the death that lives in each one of us.

Some time later, he came across a similar thought in one of Flaubert's letters to Louise Colet (August 1846) and was struck by the parallel: ". . . I always sense the future, the antithesis of everything is always before my eyes. I have never seen a child without thinking that it would grow old, nor a cradle without thinking of a grave. The sight of a naked woman makes me imagine her skeleton."

Walking through the hospital corridor and hearing the man whose leg had been amputated calling out at the top of his voice: it hurts, it hurts. That summer (1979), every day for more than a month, traveling across town to the hospital, the unbearable heat. Helping his grandfather put in his false teeth. Shaving the old man's face with an electric razor. Reading him the baseball scores from the *New York Post*.

Initial statement of these themes. Further installments to follow.

Second commentary on the nature of chance.

He remembers cutting school one drizzly day in April 1962 with his friend D. and going to the Polo Grounds to see one of the first games ever played by the New York Mets. The stadium was nearly empty (attendance was eight or nine thousand), and the Mets lost soundly to the Pittsburgh Pirates. The two friends sat next to a boy from Harlem, and A. remembers the pleasant ease of the conversation among the three of them during the course of the game.

He returned to the Polo Grounds only once that season, and that was for a holiday doubleheader (Memorial Day: day of memory, day of the dead) against the Dodgers: more than fifty

thousand people in the stands, resplendent sun, and an afternoon of crazy events on the field: a triple play, inside-the-park
homeruns, double steals. He was with the same friend that day,
and they sat in a remote corner of the stadium, unlike the good
seats they had managed to sneak into for the earlier game. At
one point they left their places to go to the hot dog stand, and
there, just several rows down the concrete steps was the same
boy they had met in April, this time sitting beside his mother.
They all recognized each other and gave warm greetings, each
amazed at the coincidence of meeting again. And make no mistake: the odds against this meeting were astronomical. Like the
two friends, A. and D., the boy now sitting with his mother had
not been to another game since that wet day in April.

Memory as a room, as a body, as a skull, as a skull that encloses
the room in which a body sits. As in the image: "a man sat
alone in his room."

"The power of memory is prodigious," observed Saint Augustine. "It is a vast, immeasurable sanctuary. Who can plumb
its depths? And yet it is a faculty of my soul. Although it is part
of my nature, I cannot understand all that I am. This means,
then, that the mind is too narrow to contain itself entirely. But
where is that part of it which it does not itself contain? Is it
somewhere outside itself and not within it? How, then, can it be
part of it, if it is not contained in it?"

The Book of Memory. Book Three.

It was in Paris, in 1965, that he first experienced the infinite
possibilities of a limited space. Through a chance encounter
with a stranger in a café, he was introduced to S. A. was just
eighteen at the time, in the summer between high school and
college, and he had never been to Paris before. These are his
earliest memories of that city, where so much of his life would
later be spent, and they are inescapably bound up with the idea
of a room.

Place Pinel in the thirteenth arrondissement, where S. lived,
was a working class neighborhood, and even then one of the
last vestiges of the old Paris—the Paris one still talks about but

which is no longer there. S. lived in a space so small that at first it seemed to defy you, to resist being entered. The presence of one person crowded the room, two people choked it. It was impossible to move inside it without contracting your body to its smallest dimensions, without contracting your mind to some infinitely small point within itself. Only then could you begin to breathe, to feel the room expand, and to watch your mind explore the excessive, unfathomable reaches of that space. For there was an entire universe in that room, a miniature cosmology that contained all that is most vast, most distant, most unknowable. It was a shrine, hardly bigger than a body, in praise of all that exists beyond the body: the representation of one man's inner world, even to the slightest detail. S. had literally managed to surround himself with the things that were inside him. The room he lived in was a dream space, and its walls were like the skin of some second body around him, as if his own body had been transformed into a mind, a breathing instrument of pure thought. This was the womb, the belly of the whale, the original site of the imagination. By placing himself in that darkness, S. had invented a way of dreaming with open eyes.

A former student of Vincent D'Indy's, S. had once been considered a highly promising young composer. For more than twenty years, however, none of his pieces had been performed in public. Naive in all things, but most especially in politics, he had made the mistake of allowing two of his larger orchestral works to be played in Paris during the war—*Symphonie de Feu* and *Hommage à Jules Verne*, each requiring more than one hundred-thirty musicians. That was in 1943, and the Nazi occupation was still at full strength. When the war ended, people concluded that S. had been a collaborator, and although nothing could have been farther from the truth, he was blackballed by the French music world—by innuendo and silent consent, never by direct confrontation. The only sign that any of his colleagues still remembered him was the annual Christmas card he received from Nadia Boulanger.

A stammerer, a child-man with a weakness for red wine, he was so lacking in guile, so ignorant of the world's malice, that he could not even begin to defend himself against his anonymous accusers. He simply withdrew, hiding behind a mask of eccentricity. He appointed himself an Orthodox priest (he was Russian), grew a long beard, dressed in a black cassock, and changed his name to the Abbaye de la Tour du Calame, all the while continuing—fitfully, between bouts of stupor—with the work of his life: a piece for three orchestras and four choruses that would take twelve days to perform. In his misery, in the totally abject conditions of his life, he would turn to A. and observe, stuttering helplessly, his gray eyes gleaming, "Everything is miraculous. There has never been an age more wonderful than this one."

The sun did not penetrate his room on the Place Pinel. He had covered his window with heavy black cloth, and what little light there was came from a few strategically placed and faintly glowing lamps. The room was hardly bigger than a second class train compartment, and it had more or less the same shape: narrow, high-ceilinged, with a single window at the far end. S. had cluttered this tiny place with a multitude of objects, the debris of an entire lifetime: books, photographs, manuscripts, private totems—everything that was of any significance to him. Shelves, densely packed with this accumulation, climbed up to the ceiling along each wall, each one sagging, tipping slightly inward, as if the slightest disturbance would loosen the structure and send the whole mass of things falling in on him. S. lived, worked, ate, and slept in his bed. Immediately to the left of him, fit snugly into the wall, was a set of small, cubbied shelves, which seemed to hold all he needed to get through the day: pens, pencils, ink, music paper, cigarette holder, radio, penknife, bottles of wine, bread, books, magnifying glass. To his right was a metal stand with a tray fastened to the top of it, which he could swing in and out, over the bed and away from it, and which he used as both his work table and his eating table. This was life as Crusoe would have lived it: shipwreck in the heart of the city. For there was nothing S. had not thought of. In his penury, he had managed to provide for himself more efficiently than many millionaires do. The evidence notwithstanding, he was a realist, even in his eccentricity. He had examined himself thoroughly enough to know what was necessary for his own survival, and he accepted these quirks as the conditions of his life. There was nothing in his attitude that was either faint-hearted or pious, nothing to suggest a hermit's renunciation. He embraced his condition with passion and joyful enthusiasm, and as A. looks back on it now, he realizes that he has never known anyone who laughed so hard and so often.

The giant composition, on which S. had spent the last fifteen years, was nowhere near completion. S. referred to it as his "work in progress," consciously echoing Joyce, whom he greatly admired, or else as the *Dodecalogue*, which he would describe as the-work-to-be-done-that-is-done-in-the-process-of-doing-it. It was unlikely that he ever imagined he would finish the piece. He seemed to accept the inevitability of his failure almost as a theological premise, and what for another man might have led to an impasse of despair was for him a source of boundless, quixotic hope. At some anterior moment, perhaps at his very darkest moment, he had made the equation between his life and his work, and now he was no longer able to distinguish between the two. Every idea fed into his work; the idea of his work gave purpose to his life. To have conceived of something within the realm of possibility—a work that could have been finished, and therefore detached from himself—would have vitiated the enterprise. The point was to fall short, but to do so only in attempting the most outlandish thing he could conjure for himself. The end result, paradoxically, was humility, a way of gaging his own insignificance in relation to God. For only in the mind of God were such dreams as S.'s possible. But by dreaming in the way he did, S. had found a way of participating in all that was beyond him, of drawing himself several inches closer to the heart of the infinite.

For more than a month during that summer of 1965, A. paid S. two or three visits a week. He knew no one else in the city, and S. therefore had become his anchor to the place. He could always count on S. to be in, to greet him with enthusiasm (Russian style; three kisses on the cheeks: left, right, left), and to be more than willing to talk. Many years later, at a time of great personal distress, he realized that what drew him continually to these meetings with S. was that they allowed him to experience, for the first time, what it felt like to have a father.

His own father was a remote, almost absent figure with whom he had very little in common. S., for his part, had two grown sons, and both had turned away from his example and adopted an aggressive, hard-nosed attitude towards the world. Beyond the natural rapport that existed between them, S. and A. drew together out of a congruent want: the one for a son who would accept him as he was, the other for a father who would accept him as he was. This was further underscored by a parallel of births: S. had been born in the same year as A.'s father; A. had been born in the same year as S.'s younger son. For A., S. satisfied his paternal hunger through a curious combination of generosity and need. He listened to him seriously and took his ambition to be a writer as the most natural thing a young man could hope to do with himself. If A.'s father, in his strange, self-enclosed manner of being in the world, had made A. feel superfluous to his life, as if nothing he did could ever have an effect on him, S., in his vulnerability and destitution, allowed A. to become necessary to him. A. brought food to him, supplied him with wine and cigarettes, made sure he did not starve—which was a true danger. For that was the point about S.: he never asked anyone for anything. He would wait for the world to come to him, entrusting his deliverance to chance. Sooner or later, someone was bound to turn up: his ex-wife, one of his sons, a friend. Even then, he would not ask. But neither would he refuse.

Each time A. arrived with a meal (usually roast chicken, from a charcuterie on the Place d'Italie), it was turned into a mock feast, an excuse for celebration. "Ah, chicken," S. would exclaim, biting into a drumstick. And then again, chewing away at it, the juice dribbling into his beard: "Ah, chicken," with an impish, self-deprecatory burst of laughter, as if acknowledging the irony of his need and the undeniable pleasure the food gave him. Everything became absurd and luminous in that laughter. The world was turned inside out, swept away, and then immediately reborn as a kind of metaphysical jest. There was no

room in that world for a man who did not have a sense of his
own ridiculousness.

Further encounters with S. Letters between Paris and New York,
a few photographs exchanged, all of this now lost. In 1967: another visit for several months. By then S. had given up his
priest's robes and was back to using his own name. But the costumes he wore on his little excursions through the streets of his
neighborhood were just as marvelous. Beret, silk shirt, scarf,
heavy corduroy pants, leather riding boots, ebony walking stick
with a silver handle: a vision of Paris via Hollywood, circa
1920. It was no accident, perhaps, that S.'s younger son became
a film producer.

In February 1971, A. returned to Paris, where he would remain for the next three and a half years. Although he was no
longer there as a visitor, which meant that more claims were
made on his time, he still saw S. on a fairly regular basis, perhaps once every other month. The bond was still there, but as
time went on A. began to wonder if it was not, in fact, a memory of that other bond, formed six years earlier, which sus-
tained this bond in the present. For it turns out that after A.
moved back to New York (July 1974), he no longer wrote any
letters to S. It was not that he did not continue to think of him.
But it was the memory of him, more than any need to carry on
contact with S. into the future, that seemed to concern A. now.
In this way he began to feel, as if palpably in his own skin, the
passage of time. It sufficed him to remember. And this, in itself,
was a startling discovery.

Even more startling to him, however, was that when he finally went back to Paris (November 1979), after an absence of
more than five years, he failed to look up S. And this in spite of
the fact that he had fully intended to do so. Every morning for
the several weeks of his visit, he would wake up and say to himself, I must make time today to see S., and then, as the day wore
on, invent an excuse for not going to see him. This reluctance,
he began to realize, was a product of fear. But fear of what? Of
walking back into his own past? Of discovering a present that
would contradict the past, and thus alter it, which in turn

would destroy the memory of the past he wanted to preserve? No, he realized, nothing so simple. Then what? Days went by, and gradually it began to come clear. He was afraid that S. was dead. Irrationally, he knew. But since A.'s father had died less than a year before, and since S. had become important to him precisely in relation to his thoughts about his father, he felt that somehow the death of one automatically entailed the death of the other. In spite of what he tried to tell himself, he actually believed this. Beyond that he thought: if I go to see S., then I will learn he is dead; but if I stay away, it will mean he is alive. By remaining absent, therefore, A. felt that he would be helping to keep S. in the world. Day after day, he walked around Paris with an image of S. in his mind. A hundred times a day, he imagined himself entering the little room on the Place Pinel. And still, he could not bring himself to go there. It was then that he realized he was living in a state of extreme duress.

Further commentary on the nature of chance.

From his last visit to S., at the end of those years in Paris (1974), a photograph has been preserved. A. and S. are standing outside, by the doorway of S.'s house. They each have an arm around the other's shoulder, and there is an unmistakeable glow of friendship and comraderie on their faces. This picture is one of the few personal tokens A. has brought with him to his room on Varick Street.

As he studies this picture now (Christmas Eve, 1979), he is reminded of another picture he used to see on the wall of S.'s room: S. as a young man, perhaps eighteen or nineteen, standing with a boy of twelve or thirteen. Same evocation of friendship, same smiles, same arms-around-the-shoulders pose. The boy, S. had told him, was the son of Marina Tsvetayeva. Marina Tsvetayeva, who stands in A.'s mind along with Mandelstam as the greatest of Russian poets. To look at this 1974 photograph for him is to imagine her impossible life, which ended when she hanged herself in 1941. For many of the years between the Civil War and her death she had lived in the Russian emigré circles in France, the same community in which S. had been raised, and he had known her and had been a friend of her son, Mur. Marina Tsvetayeva, who had written: "It may be that a better way / To conquer time and the world / Is to pass, and not to leave a trace—/ To pass, and not to leave a shadow / on the walls . . ."; who had written: "I didn't want this, not / this (but listen, quietly, / to want is what bodies do / and now we are ghosts only) . . ."; who had written: "In this most Christian of worlds / All poets are Jews."

When A. and his wife returned to New York in 1974, they moved into an apartment on Riverside Drive. Among their neighbors in the building was an old Russian doctor, Gregory Altschuller, a man well into his eighties, who still did research work at one of the city hospitals and who, along with his wife, had a great interest in literature. Dr. Altschuller's father had been Tolstoy's personal physician, and propped up on a table in the Riverside Drive apartment was an enormous photograph of the bearded writer, duly inscribed, in an equally enormous hand, to his friend and doctor. In conversations with the younger Dr. Altschuller, A. learned something that struck him as nothing less than extraordinary. In a small village outside Prague, in the dead of winter in 1925, this man had delivered Marina Tsvetayeva's son: the same son who had grown up into the boy in the photograph on S.'s wall. More than that: this was the only baby he ever delivered in his career as a doctor.

"It was night," Dr. Altschuller wrote recently, "the last day of January, 1925. . . . The snow was falling, a terrible storm which snowed-in everything. A Czech boy came running to me from the village where Tsvetayeva now lived with her family, though her husband was not with her at the time. Her daughter was also away with her father. Marina was alone.

"The boy rushed into the room and said: 'Pani Tsvetayeva wants you to come to her immediately because she's already in labor! You have to hurry, it's already on the way.' What could I say? I quickly dressed and walked through the forest, snow up to my knees, in a raging storm. I opened the door and went in. In the pale light of a lonely electric bulb I saw piles of books in one corner of the room; they nearly reached the ceiling. Days of accumulated rubbish was shoveled into another corner of the room. And there was Marina, chain-smoking in bed, baby already on

the way. Greeting me gaily: 'You're almost late!' I looked around
the room for something clean, for a piece of soap. Nothing, not a
clean handkerchief, not a piece of anything. She was lying in bed,
smoking and smiling, saying: 'I told you that you'd deliver my
baby. You came—and now it's your business, not mine'. . . .

"Everything went smoothly enough. The baby, however, was
born with the umbilical cord wrapped around his neck so
tightly that he could hardly breathe. He was blue. . . .

"I tried desperately to restore the baby's respiration and finally he started breathing; he turned from blue to pink. All this
time Marina was smoking, silent, not uttering a sound, looking
steadily at the baby, at me. . . .

"I came back the next day and then saw the child every Sunday for a good many weeks. In a letter (May 10, 1925), Marina
wrote: 'Altschuller directs everything concerning Mur with
pride and love. Before eating, Mur gets one teaspoonful of
lemon juice without sugar. He's fed according to the system of
Professor Czerny, who saved thousands of newborn children in
Germany during the war. Altschuller sees Mur every Sunday.
Percussion, auscultation, some kind of arithmetic calculation.
Then he writes down for me how to feed Mur next week, what
to give him, how much butter, how much lemon, how much
milk, how gradually to increase the amount. Every time he
comes he remembers what was given last time, without carrying
any notes. . . . Sometimes I have a crazy desire just to take his
hand and kiss it'. . . .

"The boy grew quickly and became a healthy child adored by
his mother and her friends. I saw him for the last time when he
was not yet one year old. At that time Marina moved to France
and there she lived for the next fourteen years. George (Mur's
formal name) went to school and soon became an ardent student of literature, music, and art. In 1936 his sister Alia, then in
her early twenties, left the family and France and returned to
Soviet Russia, following her father. Marina stayed now with
her very young son, alone in France . . . under extreme hard-
ship, financial and moral. In 1939 she applied for a Soviet visa
and returned to Moscow with her son. Two years later, in August 1941, her life came to a tragic end. . . .

"The war was still on. Young George Efron was at the front. 'Good-bye literature, music, school,' he wrote to his sister. He signed his letter 'Mur.' As a soldier he proved to be a courageous and fearless fighter, took part in many battles, and died in July 1944, one of hundreds of victims of a battle near the village of Druika on the Western Front. He was only twenty years old."

The Book of Memory. Book Four.

Several blank pages. To be followed by profuse illustrations. Old family photographs, for each person his own family, going back as many generations as possible. To look at these with utmost care.

Afterwards, several sequences of reproductions, beginning with the portraits Rembrandt painted of his son, Titus. To include all of them: from the view of the little boy in 1650 (golden hair, red feathered hat) to the 1655 portrait of Titus "puzzling over his lessons" (pensive, at his desk, compass dangling from his left hand, right thumb pressed against his chin) to Titus in 1658 (seventeen years old, the extraordinary red hat, and, as one commentator has written, "The artist has painted his son with the same sense of penetration usually reserved for his own features") to the last surviving canvas of Titus, from the early 1660's: "The face seems that of a weak old man ravaged with disease. Of course, we look at it with hindsight—we know that Titus will predecease his father. . . ."

To be followed by the 1602 portrait of Sir Walter Raleigh and his eight-year old son Wat (artist unknown) that hangs in the National Portrait Gallery in London. To note: the uncanny similarity of their poses. Both father and son facing forward, left hands on hips, right feet pointing out at forty-five degree angles, the left feet pointing forward, and the somber determination on the boy's face to imitate the self-confident, imperious stare of the father. To remember: that when Raleigh was released after a thirteen-year incarceration in the Tower of London (1618) and launched out on the doomed voyage to Guiana to clear his name, Wat was with him. To remember that Wat, leading a reckless military charge against the Spanish, lost his life in the jungle. Raleigh to his wife: "I never knew what sorrow meant until now." And so he went back to England, and allowed the King to chop off his head.

To be followed by more photographs, perhaps several dozen: Mallarmé's son, Anatole; Anne Frank ("This is a photo that shows me as I should always like to look. Then I would surely have a chance to go to Hollywood. But now, unfortunately, I usually look different"); Mur; the children of Cambodia; the children of Atlanta. The dead children. The children who will vanish, the children who are dead. Himmler: "I have made the decision to annihilate every Jewish child from the face of the earth." Nothing but pictures. Because, at a certain point, the words lead one to conclude that it is no longer possible to speak. Because these pictures are the unspeakable.

He has spent the greater part of his adult life walking through cities, many of them foreign. He has spent the greater part of his adult life hunched over a small rectangle of wood, concentrating on an even smaller rectangle of white paper. He has spent the greater part of his adult life standing up and sitting down and pacing back and forth. These are the limits of the known world. He listens. When he hears something, he begins to listen again. Then he waits. He watches and waits. And when he begins to see something, he watches and waits again. These are the limits of the known world.

The room. Brief mention of the room and/or the dangers lurking inside it. As in the image: Hölderlin in his room.

To revive the memory of that mysterious, three-month journey on foot, crossing the mountains of the Massif Central alone, his fingers gripped tightly around the pistol in his pocket; that journey from Bordeaux to Stuttgart (hundreds of miles) that preceded his first mental breakdown in 1802.

"Dear friend . . . I have not written to you for a long time, and meanwhile have been in France and have seen the sad, lonely earth; the shepherds and shepherdesses of southern France and individual beauties, men and women, who grew up in fear of political uncertainty and of hunger. . . . The mighty element, the fire of heaven and the silence of the people, their life in nature, their confinedness and their contentment, moved me continually, and as one says of heroes, I can well say of myself that Apollo has struck me."

Arriving in Stuttgart, "deathly pale, very thin, with hollow wild eyes, long hair and a beard, and dressed like a beggar," he stood before his friend Matthison and spoke one word only: "Hölderlin."

Six months later, his beloved Suzette was dead. By 1806, schizophrenia, and thereafter, for thirty-six years, fully half his life, he lived alone in the tower built for him by Zimmer, the carpenter from Tubingen—*zimmer*, which in German means *room*.

TO ZIMMER

> The lines of life are various as roads or as
> The limits of the mountains are, and what we are
> Down here, in harmonies, in recompense,
> In peace for ever, a god will finish there.

Toward the end of Hölderlin's life, a visitor to the tower mentioned Suzette's name. The poet replied: "Ah, my Diotima. Don't speak to me about my Diotima. Thirteen sons she bore me. One is Pope, another is the Sultan, the third is the Emperor of Russia. . . ." And then: "Do you know what happened to her? She went mad, she did, mad, mad, mad."

During those years, it is said, Hölderlin rarely went out. When he did leave his room, it was only to take aimless walks through the countryside, filling his pockets with stones and picking flowers, which he would later tear to shreds. In town, the students laughed at him, and children ran away in fear whenever he approached to greet them. Towards the end, his mind became so muddled that he began to call himself by different names—Scardinelli, Killalusimeno—and once, when a visitor was slow to leave his room, he showed him the door and said, with a finger raised in warning, "I am the Lord God."

In recent years, there has been renewed speculation about Hölderlin's life in that room. One man contends that Hölderlin's

madness was feigned, and that in response to the stultifying political reaction that overwhelmed Germany following the
French revolution, the poet withdrew from the world. He lived,
so to speak, underground in the tower. According to this theory, all of the writings of Hölderlin's madness (1806–1843)
were in fact composed in a secret, revolutionary code. There is
even a play that expands upon this idea. In the final scene of
that work, the young Marx pays Hölderlin a visit in his tower.
We are led to presume from this encounter that it was the old
and dying poet who inspired Marx to write *The Economic
and Philosophical Manuscripts of 1844*. If this were so, then
Hölderlin would not only have been the greatest German poet
of the nineteenth century, but also a central figure in the history of political thought: the link between Hegel and Marx.
For it is a documented fact that as young men Hölderlin and
Hegel were friends. They were students together at the semi-
nary in Tübingen.

Speculations of this sort, however, strike A. as tedious. He
has no difficulty in accepting Hölderlin's presence in the room.
He would even go so far as to say that Hölderlin could not have
survived anywhere else. If not for Zimmer's generosity and
kindness, it is possible that Hölderlin's life would have ended
prematurely. To withdraw into a room does not mean that one
has been blinded. To be mad does not mean that one has been
struck dumb. More than likely, it is the room that restored
Hölderlin to life, that gave him back whatever life it was left for
him to live. As Jerome commented on the Book of Jonah, gloss-
ing the passage that tells of Jonah in the belly of the whale:
"You will note that where you would think should be the end of
Jonah, there was his safety."

"The image of man has eyes," wrote Hölderlin, during the
first year of his life in that room, "whereas the moon has light.
King Oedipus has an eye too many perhaps. The sufferings of
this man, they seem indescribable, unspeakable, inexpressible.
If the drama represents something like this, that is why. But
what comes over me as I think of you now? Like brooks the end
of something sweeps me away, which expands like Asia. Of
course, this affliction, Oedipus has it too. Of course, that is

why. Did Hercules suffer too? Indeed. . . . For to fight with God, like Hercules, that is an affliction. And immortality amidst the envy of this life, to share in that, is an affliction too. But this is also an affliction, when a man is covered with freckles, to be wholly covered with many a spot! The beautiful sun does that: for it rears up all things. It leads young men along their course with the allurements of its beams as though with roses. The afflictions that Oedipus bore seem like this, as when a poor man complains there is something he lacks. Son of Laios, poor stranger in Greece! Life is death, and death is a kind of life."

The room. Counter-argument to the above. Or: reasons for being in the room.

The Book of Memory. Book Five.

Two months after his father's death (January 1979), A.'s marriage collapsed. The problems had been brewing for some time, and at last the decision was made to separate. If it was one thing for him to accept this break-up, to be miserable about it and yet to understand that it was inevitable, it was quite another thing for him to swallow the consequences it entailed: to be separated from his son. The thought of it was intolerable to him.

He moved into his room on Varick Street in early spring. For the next few months he shuttled between that room and the house in Dutchess County where he and his wife had been living for the past three years. During the week: solitude in the city; on the weekends: visits to the country, one hundred miles away, where he slept in what was now his former work room and played with his son, not yet two years old, and read to him from the treasured books of the period: *Let's Go Trucks, Caps for Sale, Mother Goose.*

Shortly after he moved into the Varick Street room, the six-year old Etan Patz disappeared from the streets of that same neighborhood. Everywhere A. turned, there was a photograph of the boy (on lampposts, in shop windows, on blank brick walls), headlined by the words: LOST CHILD. Because the face of this child did not differ drastically from the face of his own child (and even if it had, it might not have mattered), every time he saw the photograph of this face he was made to think of his own son—and in precisely these terms: lost child. Etan Patz had been sent downstairs one morning by his mother to wait for the school bus (the first day following a long bus driver strike, and the boy had been eager to do this one little thing on his own, to make this small gesture of independence), and then was not seen again. Whatever it was that happened to him, it happened without a trace. He could have been kidnapped, he could have been murdered, or perhaps he simply wandered off and came to his death in a place where no one could see him. The only thing that can be said with any certainty is that he vanished—as if from the face of the earth. The newspapers made much of this story (interviews with the parents, interviews with the detectives assigned to the case, articles about the boy's personality: what games he liked to play, what foods he liked to eat), and A. began to realize that the presence of this disaster—superimposed on his own and admittedly much smaller disaster—was inescapable. Each thing that fell before his eyes seemed to be no more than an image of what was inside him. The days went by, and each day a little more of the pain inside him was dragged out into the open. A sense of loss took hold of him, and it would not let go. And there were times when this loss was so great, and so suffocating, that he thought it would never let go.

Some weeks later, at the beginning of summer. A radiant New York June: clarity of the light falling on the bricks; blue, transparent skies, zeroing to an azure that would have charmed even Mallarmé.

A.'s grandfather (on his mother's side) was slowly beginning to die. Only a year before he had performed magic tricks at A.'s son's first birthday party, but now, at eighty-five, he was so weak that he could no longer stand without support, could no longer move without an effort of will so intense that merely to think of moving was enough to exhaust him. There was a family conference at the doctor's office, and the decision was made to send him to Doctor's Hospital on East End Avenue and Eighty-eighth Street (the same hospital in which his wife had died of amniotropic lateral sclerosis—Lou Gehrig's disease—eleven years earlier). A. was at that conference, as were his mother and his mother's sister, his grandfather's two children. Because neither of the women could remain in New York, it was agreed that A. would be responsible for everything. A.'s mother had to return home to California to take care of her own gravely ill husband, while A.'s aunt was about to go to Paris to visit her first grandchild, the recently born daughter of her only son. Everything, it seemed, had quite literally become a matter of life and death. At which point, A. suddenly found himself thinking (perhaps because his grandfather had always reminded him of W.C. Fields) of a scene from the 1932 Fields film, *Million Dollar Legs:* Jack Oakey runs frantically to catch up with a departing stage coach and beseeches the driver to stop; "It's a matter of life and death!" he shouts. And the driver calmly and cynically replies: "What isn't?"

During this family conference A. could see the fear on his grandfather's face. At one point the old man caught his eye and gestured up to the wall beside the doctor's desk, which was covered with laminated plaques, framed certificates, awards, degrees, and testimonials, and gave a knowing nod, as if to say, "Pretty impressive, eh? This guy will take good care of me." The old man had always been taken in by pomp of this sort. "I've just received a letter from the president of the Chase Manhattan Bank," he would say, when in fact it was nothing more than a form letter. That day in the doctor's office, however, it was painful for A. to see it: the old man's refusal to recognize the thing that was looking him straight in the eyes. "I feel good about all this, doctor," his grandfather said. "I know you're going to get me better again." And yet, almost against his will, A. found himself admiring this capacity for blindness. Later that day, he helped his grandfather pack a small satchel of things to take to the hospital. The old man tossed three or four of his magic tricks into the bag. "Why are you bothering with those?" A. asked. "So I can entertain the nurses," his grandfather replied, "in case things get dull."

A. decided to stay in his grandfather's apartment for as long as the old man was in the hospital. The place could not remain empty (someone had to pay the bills, collect the mail, water the plants), and it was bound to be more comfortable than the room on Varick Street. Above all, the illusion had to be maintained that the old man was coming back. Until there was death, there was always the possibility there would not be death, and this chance, slight though it was, had to be credited.

A. remained in that apartment for the next six or seven weeks. It was the same place he had been visiting since earliest childhood: that tall, squat, oddly shaped building that stands on the corner of Central Park South and Columbus Circle. He wondered how many hours he had spent as a boy looking out at the traffic as it wove around the statue of Christopher Columbus. Through those same sixth floor windows he had watched the Thanksgiving Day parades, seen the construction of the Colosseum, spent entire afternoons counting the people as they walked by on the streets below. Now he was surrounded by this place again, with the Chinese telephone table, his grandmother's glass menagerie, and the old humidor. He had walked straight back into his childhood.

A. continued to hope for a reconciliation with his wife. When she agreed to come to the city with their son to stay at the apartment, he felt that perhaps a real change would be possible. Cut off from the objects and cares of their own life, they seemed to settle in nicely to these neutral surroundings. But neither one of them was ready at that point to admit that this was not an illusion, an act of memory coupled with an act of groundless hope.

Every afternoon A. would travel to the hospital by boarding two buses, spend an hour or two with his grandfather, and then return by the same route he had come. This arrangement worked for about ten days. Then the weather changed. An excruciating heat fell on New York, and the city became a nightmare of sweat, exhaustion, and noise. None of this did the little boy any good (cooped up in the apartment with a sputtering air conditioner, or else traipsing through the steamy streets with his mother), and when the weather refused to break (record humidity for several weeks running), A. and his wife decided that she and the boy should return to the country.

He stayed on in his grandfather's apartment alone. Each day became a repetition of the day before. Conversations with the doctor, the trip to the hospital, hiring and firing private nurses, listening to his grandfather's complaints, straightening the pillows under his head. There was a horror that went through him each time he glimpsed the old man's flesh. The emaciated limbs, the shriveled testicles, the body that had shrunk to less than a hundred pounds. This was a once corpulent man, whose proud, well-stuffed belly had preceded his every step through the world, and now he was hardly there. If A. had experienced one kind of death earlier in the year, a death so sudden that even as it gave him over to death it deprived him of the knowledge of that death, now he was experiencing death of another kind, and it was this slow, mortal exhaustion, this letting go of life in the heart of life, that finally taught him the thing he had known all along.

Nearly every day there was a phone call from his grandfather's former secretary, a woman who had worked in the office for more than twenty years. After his grandmother's death, she had become the steadiest of his grandfather's lady companions, the respectable woman he trotted out for public view on formal occasions: family gatherings, weddings, funerals. Each time she called, she would make copious inquiries about his grandfather's health, and then ask A. to arrange for her to visit the hospital. The problem was her own bad health. Although not old (late sixties at most), she suffered from Parkinson's disease, and for some time had been living in a nursing home in the Bronx. After numerous conversations (her voice so faint over the telephone that it took all of A.'s powers of concentration to hear even half of what she said), he finally agreed to meet her in front of the Metropolitan Museum, where a special bus from the nursing home deposited ambulatory patients once a week for an afternoon in Manhattan. On that particular day, for the first time in nearly a month, it rained. A. arrived in advance of the appointed time, and then, for more than an hour, stood on the museum steps, keeping his head dry with a newspaper, on the lookout for the woman. At last, deciding to give up, he made one final tour of the area. It was then that he found her: a block or two up Fifth Avenue, standing under a pathetic sapling, as if to protect herself from the rain, a clear plastic bonnet on her head, leaning on her walking stick, body bent forward, all of her rigid, afraid to take a step, staring down at the wet sidewalk. Again that feeble voice, and A. almost pressing his ear against her mouth to hear her—only to glean some paltry and insipid remark: the bus driver had forgotten to shave, the newspaper had not been delivered. A. had always been bored by this woman, and even when she had been well he had cringed at having to spend more than five minutes in her company. Now he found himself almost angry at her, resenting the way in which she seemed to expect him to pity her. He lashed out at her in his mind for being such an abject creature of self-absorption.

More than twenty minutes went by before he could get a cab. And then the endless ordeal of walking her to the curb and putting her into the taxi. Her shoes scraping on the pavement: one inch and then pause; another inch and then pause; another inch and then another inch. He held her arm and did his best to encourage her along. When they reached the hospital and he finally managed to disentangle her from the back seat of the cab, they began the slow journey toward the entrance. Just in front of the door, at the very instant A. thought they were going to make it, she froze. She had suddenly been gripped by the fear that she could not move, and therefore she could not move. No matter what A. said to her, no matter how gently he tried to coax her forward, she would not budge. People were going in and out—doctors, nurses, visitors—and there they stood, A. and the helpless woman, locked in the middle of that human traffic. A. told her to wait where she was (as if she could have done anything else), and went into the lobby, where he found an empty wheelchair, which he snatched out from under the eyes of a suspicious woman administrator. Then he eased his helpless companion into the chair and bustled her through the lobby toward the elevator, fending off the shouts of the administrator: "Is she a patient? Is that woman a patient? Wheelchairs are for patients only."

When he wheeled her into his grandfather's room, the old man was drowsing, neither asleep nor awake, lolling in a torpor at the edge of consciousness. He revived enough at the sound of their entering to perceive their presence, and then, at last understanding what had happened, smiled for the first time in weeks. Tears suddenly filled his eyes. He took hold of the woman's hand and said to A., as if addressing the entire world (but feebly, ever so feebly): "Shirley is my sweetheart. Shirley is the one I love."

In late July, A. decided to spend a weekend out of the city. He wanted to see his son, and he needed a break from the heat and the hospital. His wife came into New York, leaving the boy with her parents. What they did in the city that day he cannot remember, but by late afternoon they had made it out to the beach in Connecticut where the boy had spent the day with his grandparents. A. found his son sitting on a swing, and the first words out of the boy's mouth (having been coached all afternoon by his grandmother) were surprising in their lucidity. "I'm very happy to see you, daddy," he said.

At the same time, the voice sounded strange to A. The boy seemed to be short of breath, and he spoke each word in a staccato of separate syllables. A. had no doubt that something was wrong. He insisted that they all leave the beach at once and go back to the house. Although the boy was in good spirits, this curious, almost mechanical voice continued to speak through him, as though he were a ventriloquist's dummy. His breathing was extremely rapid: heaving torso, in and out, in and out, like the breathing of a little bird. Within an hour, A. and his wife were looking down a list of local pediatricians, trying to reach one who was in (it was dinner hour on Friday night). On the fifth or sixth try they got hold of a young woman doctor who had recently taken over a practice in town. By some fluke, she happened to be in her office at that hour, and she told them to come right over. Either because she was new at her work, or because she had an excitable nature, her examination of the little

boy threw A. and his wife into a panic. She sat the boy up on
the table, listened to his chest, counted his breaths per minute,
observed his flared nostrils, the slightly bluish tint to the skin of
his face. Then a mad rush about the office, trying to rig up a
complicated breathing device: a vapor machine with a hood,
reminiscent of a nineteenth century camera. But the boy would
not keep his head under the hood, and the hissing of the cold
steam frightened him. The doctor then tried a shot of adrenalin.
"We'll try this one," she said, "and if it doesn't work we'll give
him another." She waited a few minutes, went through the
breath-rate calculations again, and then gave him the second
shot. Still no effect. "That's it," she said. "We'll have to take
him to the hospital." She made the necessary phone call, and
with a furious energy that seemed to gather up everything into
her small body, told A. and his wife how to follow her to the
hospital, where to go, what to do, and then led them outside,
where they left in separate cars. Her diagnosis was pneumonia
with asthmatic complications—which, after X-rays and more
sophisticated tests at the hospital, turned out to be the case.

The boy was put in a special room in the children's ward,
pricked and poked by nurses, held down screaming as liquid
medicine was poured into his throat, hooked up to an I.V. line,
and placed in a crib that was then covered by a clear plastic
tent—into which a mist of cold oxygen was pumped from a
valve in the wall. The boy remained in this tent for three days
and three nights. His parents were allowed to be with him con-
tinuously, and they took turns sitting beside the boy's crib, head
and arms under the tent, reading him books, telling him stories,
playing games, while the other sat in a small reading room reserved for adults, watching the faces of the other parents whose
children were in the hospital: none of these strangers daring to
talk to each other, since they were all thinking of only one
thing, and to speak of it would only have made it worse.

It was exhausting for the boy's parents, since the medicine
dripping into his veins was composed essentially of adrenalin.
This charged him with extra doses of energy—above and beyond the normal energy of a two-year old—and much of their
time was spent in trying to calm him down, restraining him

from breaking out of the tent. For A. this was of little consequence. The fact of the boy's illness, the fact that had they not taken him to the doctor in time he might actually have died, (and the horror that washed over him when he thought: what if he and his wife had decided to spend the night in the city, entrusting the boy to his grandparents—who, in their old age, had ceased to be observant of details, and who, in fact, had not noticed the boy's strange breathing at the beach and had scoffed at A. when he first mentioned it), the fact of all these things made the struggle to keep the boy calm as nothing to A. Merely to have contemplated the possibility of the boy's death, to have had the thought of his death thrown in his face at the doctor's office, was enough for him to treat the boy's recovery as a sort of resurrection, a miracle dealt to him by the cards of chance.

His wife, however, began to show the strain. At one point she walked out to A., who was in the adult sitting room, and said: "I give up, I can't handle him anymore"—and there was such resentment in her voice against the boy, such an anger of exasperation, that something inside A. fell to pieces. Stupidly, cruelly, he wanted to punish his wife for such selfishness, and in that one instant all the newly won harmony that had been growing between them for the past month vanished: for the first time in all their years together, he had turned against her. He stormed out of the room and went to his son's bedside.

The modern nothingness. Interlude on the force of parallel lives.

In Paris that fall he attended a small dinner party given by a friend of his, J., a well-known French writer. There was another American among the guests, a scholar who specialized in modern French poetry, and she spoke to A. of a book she was in the process of editing: the selected writings of Mallarmé. Had A., she wondered, ever translated any Mallarmé?

The fact was that he had. More than five years earlier, shortly after moving into the apartment on Riverside Drive, he had translated a number of the fragments Mallarmé wrote at the bedside of his dying son, Anatole, in 1879. These were short works of the greatest obscurity: notes for a poem that never came to be written. They were not even discovered until the late 1950s. In 1974, A. had done rough translation drafts of thirty or forty of them and then had put the manuscript away. When he returned from Paris to his room on Varick Street (December 1979, exactly one hundred years after Mallarmé had scribbled those death notes to his son), he dug out the folder that contained the handwritten drafts and began to work up final versions of his translations. These were later published in the *Paris Review*, along with a photograph of Anatole in a sailor suit. From his prefatory note: "On October 6, 1879, Mallarmé's only son, Anatole, died at the age of eight after a long illness. The disease, diagnosed as child's rheumatism, had slowly spread from limb to limb and eventually overtaken the boy's entire body. For several months Mallarmé and his wife had sat helplessly at Anatole's bedside as doctors tried various remedies and administered unsuccessful treatments. The boy was shuttled from the city to the country and back to the city again. On August 22 Mallarmé wrote to his friend Henry Ronjon 'of the struggle between life and death our poor little darling is going through . . . But the real pain is that this little being might vanish. I confess that it is too much for me; I cannot bring myself to face this idea.' "

It was precisely this idea, A. realized, that moved him to return to these texts. The act of translating them was not a literary exercise. It was a way for him to relive his own moment of panic in the doctor's office that summer: it is too much for me, I cannot face it. For it was only at that moment, he later came to realize, that he had finally grasped the full scope of his own fatherhood: the boy's life meant more to him than his own; if dying were necessary to save his son, he would be willing to die. And it was therefore only in that moment of fear that he had become, once and for all, the father of his son. Translating those forty or so fragments by Mallarmé was perhaps an insignificant thing, but in his own mind it had become the equivalent of offering a prayer of thanks for the life of his son. A prayer to what? To nothing perhaps. To his sense of life. To *the modern nothingness*.

you can, with your little
hands, drag me
into the grave—you
have the right—
—I
who follow you, I
let myself go—
—but if you
wish, the two
of us, let us make . . .

an alliance
a hymen, superb
—and the life
remaining in me
I will use for——
                         *

no—nothing
to do with the great
deaths—etc.
—as long as we
go on living, he
lives—in us

it will only be after our
death that he will be dead
—and the bells
of the Dead will toll for
                              him
                         *

sail—
navigates
river,
your life that
goes by, that flows
                         *

Setting sun
and wind
    now vanished, and
wind of *nothing*
that breathes
(here, the modern
? nothingness)
             *

death—whispers softly
—I am no one—
I do not even know who I am
(for the dead do not
know they are
dead—, nor even that they
                      die

—for children
at least
    —or

heroes—sudden
deaths

for otherwise
my beauty is
made *of last*
moments—
lucidity, beauty
face—of what would be

me, without myself
            *

Oh! you understand
that if I consent
to live—to seem
to forget you—

         it is to
         feed my pain
         —and so that this apparent
         forgetfulness
                 can spring forth more
         horribly in tears, at

         some random
         moment, in
         the middle of this
         life, when you
         appear to me
                      *

         true mourning in
             the apartment
         —not cemetery—

                furniture
                      *

         to find *only*
         absence—
         —in presence
         of little clothes
         —etc—
                      *

             no—I will not
         give up
             nothingness

             father—I
         feel nothingness
             invade me

Brief commentary on the word "radiance."
   He first heard this word used in connection with his son

when he had shown a photograph of the boy to his good friend, R., an American poet who had lived for eight years in Amsterdam. They were drinking in a bar that night, surrounded by a press of bodies and loud music. A. pulled the snapshot out of his wallet and handed it to R., who studied the picture for a long time. Then he turned to A., a little drunk, and said with great emotion in his voice: "He has the same radiance as Titus."

About one year later, shortly after the publication of "A Tomb for Anatole" in the *Paris Review*, A. happened to be visiting R. R. (who had grown extremely fond of A.'s son) explained to A.: "An extraordinary thing happened to me today. I was in a bookstore, leafing through various magazines, and I happened to open the *Paris Review* to a photograph of Mallarmé's son. For a second I thought it was your son. The resemblance was that striking."

A. replied: "But those were my translations. I was the one who made them put in that picture. Didn't you know that?"

And then R. said: "I never got that far. I was so struck by the picture that I had to close the magazine. I put it back on the shelf and then walked out of the store."

His grandfather lasted another two or three weeks. A. returned to the apartment overlooking Columbus Circle, his son now out of danger, his marriage now at a permanent standstill. These were probably the worst days of all for him. He could not work, he could not think. He began to neglect himself, ate only noxious foods (frozen dinners, pizza, take-out Chinese noodles), and left the apartment to its own devices: dirty clothes strewn in a bedroom corner, unwashed dishes piled in the kitchen sink. Lying on the couch, smoking cigarette after cigarette, he would watch old movies on television and read second-rate mystery novels. He did not try to reach any of his friends. The one person he did call—a girl he had met in Paris when he was eighteen—had moved to Colorado.

One night, for no particular reason, he went out to wander around the lifeless neighborhood of the West Fifties and walked into a topless bar. As he sat there at his table drinking a beer, he suddenly found himself sitting next to a voluptuously naked young woman. She sidled up to him and began to describe all the lewd things she would do to him if he paid her to go to "the back room." There was something so openly humorous and matter-of-fact about her approach that he finally agreed to her proposition. The best thing, they decided, would be for her to suck his penis, since she claimed an extraordinary talent for this activity. And indeed, she threw herself into it with an enthusiasm that fairly astonished him. As he came in her mouth a few moments later, with a long and throbbing flood of semen, he had this vision, at just that second, which has continued to radiate inside him: that each ejaculation contains several billion sperm cells—or roughly the same number as there are people in the world—which means that, in himself, each man holds the potential of an entire world. And what would happen, could it happen, is the full range of possibilities: a spawn of idiots and geniuses, of the beautiful and the deformed, of saints, catatonics, thieves, stock brokers, and high-wire artists. Each man, therefore, is the entire world, bearing within his genes a memory of all mankind. Or, as Leibniz put it: "Every living substance is a perpetual living mirror of the universe." For the fact is, we are of the same stuff that came into being with the first explosion of the first spark in the infinite emptiness of space. Or so he said to himself, at that moment, as his penis exploded into the mouth of that naked woman, whose name he has now forgotten. He thought: the irreducible monad. And then, as though taking hold of it at last, he thought of the furtive, microscopic cell that had fought its way up through his wife's body, some three years earlier, to become his son.

Otherwise nothing. He languished. He sweltered in the summer heat. Like some latter-day Oblomov curled on his couch, he did not move unless he had to.

There was a cable television in his grandfather's apartment, with more channels than A. had ever known existed. Whenever he turned it on, there seemed to be a baseball game in progress. Not only was he able to follow the Yankees and Mets of New York, but the Red Sox of Boston, the Phillies of Philadelphia, and the Braves of Atlanta. Not to speak of the little bonuses occasionally provided during the afternoon: the games from the Japanese major leagues, for example (and his fascination with the constant beating of drums during the course of the game), or, even more strangely, the Little League championships from Long Island. To immerse himself in these games was to feel his mind striving to enter a place of pure form. Despite the agitation on the field, baseball offered itself to him as an image of that which does not move, and therefore a place where his mind could be at rest, secure in its refuge against the mutabilities of the world.

He had spent his entire childhood playing it. From the first muddy days in early March to the last frozen afternoons of late October. He had played well, with an almost obsessive devotion. Not only had it given him a feeling for his own possibilities, convinced him that he was not entirely hopeless in the eyes of others, but it had been the thing that drew him out from the solitary enclosures of his early childhood. It had initiated him into the world of the other, but at the same time it was something he could also keep within himself. Baseball was a terrain rich in potential for reverie. He fantasized about it continually, projecting himself into a New York Giants uniform and trotting out to his position at third base in the Polo Grounds, with the crowd cheering wildly at the mention of his name over the loudspeakers. Day after day, he would come home from school and throw a tennis ball against the steps of his house, pretending that each gesture was a part of the World Series game unfolding in his head. It always came down to two outs in the bottom of the ninth, a man on base, the Giants trailing by one. He was always the batter, and he always hit the game-winning homerun.

As he sat through those long summer days in his grandfather's apartment, he began to see that the power of baseball was for him the power of memory. Memory in both senses of the word: as a catalyst for remembering his own life and as an artificial structure for ordering the historical past. 1960, for example, was the year Kennedy was elected president; it was also the year of A.'s Bar Mitzvah, the year he supposedly reached manhood. But the first image that springs to his mind when 1960 is mentioned is Bill Mazeroski's homerun that beat the Yankees in the World Series. He can still see the ball soaring over the Forbes Field fence—that high, dark barrier, so densely cluttered with white numbers—and by recalling the sensations of that moment, that abrupt and stunning instant of pleasure, he is able to re-enter his own past, to stand in a world that would otherwise be lost to him.

He reads in a book: since 1893 (the year before his grandfather was born), when the pitcher's mound was moved back ten feet, the shape of the field has not changed. The diamond is a part of our consciousness. Its pristine geometry of white lines, green grass, and brown dirt is an icon as familiar as the stars and stripes. As opposed to just about everything else in American life during this century, baseball has remained constant. Except for a few minor alterations (artificial turf, designated hitters), the game as it is played today is remarkably similar to the one played by Wee Willie Keeler and the old Baltimore Orioles: those long dead young men of the photographs, with their handlebar moustaches and heroic poses.

What happens today is merely a variation on what happened yesterday. Yesterday echoes today, and tomorrow will foreshadow what happens next year. Professional baseball's past is intact. There is a record of every game played, a statistic for every hit, error, and base on balls. One can measure performances against each other, compare players and teams, speak of the dead as if they were still alive. To play the game as a child is simultaneously to imagine playing it as an adult, and the power of this fantasy is present in even the most casual pick-up game. How many hours of his boyhood, A. wonders, were spent trying to imitate Stan Musial's batting stance (feet together, knees bent, back hunched over in a taut French curve) or the basket catches of Willie Mays? Reciprocally, for those who grow up to be professionals, there is an awareness that they are living out their childhood dreams—in effect, being paid to remain children. Nor should the depth of those dreams be minimized. In his own Jewish childhood, A. can remember confusing the last words of the Passover Seder, "Next year in Jerusalem," with the ever-hopeful refrain of disappointed fandom, "Wait till next year," as if the one were a commentary on the other: to win the pennant was to enter the promised land. Baseball had somehow become entangled in his mind with the religious experience.

It was just then, as A. was beginning to sink into this baseball quicksand, that Thurman Munson was killed. A. noted that Munson was the first Yankee captain since Lou Gehrig, that his grandmother had died of Lou Gehrig's disease, and that his grandfather's death would come quickly in the wake of Munson's.

The newspapers were filled with articles about the catcher. A. had always admired Munson's play on the field: the quick bat flicking singles to right, the stumpy body chugging around the bases, the anger that seemed to consume him as he went about his business behind the plate. Now A. was moved to learn of Munson's work with children and the troubles he had had with his own hyperactive son. Everything seemed to be repeating itself. Reality was a Chinese box, an infinite series of containers within containers. For here again, in the most unlikely of places, the theme had reappeared: the curse of the absent father. It seemed that Munson himself was the only one who had the power to calm down the little boy. Whenever he was at home, the boy's outbursts stopped, his frenzies abated. Munson was learning how to fly a plane so that he could go home more often during the baseball season to be with his son, and it was the plane that killed him.

Inevitably, A.'s memories of baseball were connected with his memories of his grandfather. It was his grandfather who had taken him to his first game, had talked to him about the old players, had shown him that baseball was as much about talk as it was about watching. As a little boy, A. would be dropped off at the office on Fifty-seventh Street, play around with the typewriters and adding machines until his grandfather was ready to leave, and then walk out with him for a leisurely stroll down Broadway. The ritual always included a few rounds of Pokerino in one of the amusement arcades, a quick lunch, and then the subway—to one of the city ball parks. Now, with his grandfather disappearing into death, they continued to talk about baseball. It was the one subject they could still come to as equals. Each time he visited the hospital, A. would buy a copy of the *New York Post*, and then sit by the old man's bed, reading to him about the games of the day before. It was his last contact with the outside world, and it was painless, a series of coded messages he could understand with his eyes closed. Anything else would have been too much.

Toward the very end, with a voice that could barely produce a sound, his grandfather told him that he had begun to remember his life. He had been dredging up the days of his Toronto boyhood, reliving events that had taken place as far back as eighty years ago: defending his younger brother against a gang of bullies, delivering bread on Friday afternoon to the Jewish families in the neighborhood, all the trivial, long-forgotten things that now, coming back to him as he lay immobilized in bed, took on the importance of spiritual illuminations. "Lying here gives me a chance to remember," he told A., as if this were a new power he had discovered in himself. A. could sense the pleasure it gave him. Little by little, it had begun to dominate the fear that had been in his grandfather's face these past weeks. Memory was the only thing keeping him alive, and it was as though he wanted to hold off death for as long as possible in order to go on remembering.

He knew, and yet he would not say he knew. Until the final week, he continued to talk about returning to his apartment, and not once was the word "death" mentioned. Even on the last day, he waited until the last possible moment to say good-bye. A. was leaving, walking through the door after a visit, when his grandfather called him back. Again, A. stood beside the bed. The old man took hold of his hand and squeezed as hard as he could. Then: a long, long moment. At last, A. bent down and kissed his grandfather's face. Neither one of them said a word.

A. remembers a schemer, a maker of deals, a man of bizarre and grandiose optimisms. Who else, after all, could have named his daughter Queenie with a straight face? But at her birth he had declared, "she'll be a queen," and could not resist the temptation. He thrived on bluff, the symbolic gesture, on being the life of the party. Lots of jokes, lots of cronies, an impeccable sense of timing. He gambled on the sly, cheated on his wife (the older he got, the younger the girls), and never lost his taste for any of it. His locutions were particularly splendid. A towel was never just a towel, but a "Turkish towel." A taker of drugs was a "dope fiend." Nor would he ever say "I saw . . . ," but rather, "I've had an opportunity to observe. . . ." In so doing, he managed to inflate the world, to turn it into a more compelling and exotic place for himself. He played the bigshot and reveled in the side-effects of the pose: the headwaiters calling him Mr. B., the delivery boys smiling at his excessive tips, the whole world tipping its hat to him. He had come down to New York from Canada just after the First World War, a poor Jewish boy on the make, and in the end he had done all right for himself. New York was his passion, and in his last years he refused to move away, resisting his daughter's offer of a life in sunny California with these words, which became a popular refrain: "I can't leave New York. This is where the action is."

A. remembers a day when he was four or five. His grandparents came for a visit, and his grandfather did a magic trick for him, some little thing he had found in a novelty shop. On the next visit, when he failed to show up with a new trick, A. raised a fuss of disappointment. From then on there was always a new piece of magic: disappearing coins, silk scarves produced from thin air, a machine that turned strips of blank paper into money, a big rubber ball that became five little rubber balls when you squeezed it in your hand, a cigarette extinguished in a handkerchief that made no burn, a pitcher of milk poured into a cone of newspaper that made no spill. What had started out as a curiosity to amuse his grandson became a genuine calling for him. He turned himself into an accomplished amateur magician, a deft sleight-of-hand artist, and he took special pride in his membership card from the Magician's Guild. He appeared at each of A.'s childhood birthday parties with his magic and went on performing until the last year of his life, touring the senior citizen clubs of New York with one of his lady friends (a blowsy woman with a pile of fake red hair) who would sing a song, accompanying herself on the accordion, that introduced him as the Great Zavello. It was only natural. His life was so steeped in the hocus-pocus of illusion, he had pulled off so many business deals by making people believe in him (convincing them that something not there was actually there, and vice versa) that it was a small matter for him to step up on stage and fool them in a more formal way. He had the ability to make people pay attention to him, and it was clear to everyone who saw him how delighted he was to be the center of their attention. No one is less cynical than a magician. He knows, and everyone else knows, that everything he does is a sham. The trick is not really to deceive them, but to delight them into wanting to be deceived: so that for the space of a few minutes the grip of cause-and-effect is loosened, the laws of nature countermanded. As Pascal put it in the *Pensées:* "It is not possible to have reasonable grounds for not believing in miracles."

A.'s grandfather, however, did not content himself merely with magic. He was equally fond of jokes, which he called "stories"—all of them written down in a little notebook that he carried around in his coat pocket. At some point during every family gathering, he would take out the notebook, skim through it quickly in some corner of the room, put it back in his pocket, sit down in a chair, and then launch into an hour's worth of verbal nonsense. Here, too, the memory is of laughter. Not, as with S., a laughter bursting from the belly, but a laughter that meandered outward from the lungs, a long sing-song loop of sound that began as a wheeze and dispersed, gradually, into a fainter and fainter chromatic whistle. That, too, is how A. would like to remember him: sitting in that chair and making everyone laugh.

His grandfather's greatest stunt, though, was neither a magic trick nor a joke, but a kind of extra-sensory voodoo that kept everyone in the family baffled for years. It was a game called the Wizard. A.'s grandfather would take out a deck of cards, ask someone to pick a card, any card, and hold it up for everyone to see. The five of hearts. Then he would go to the phone, dial a number, and ask to speak to the Wizard. That's right, he would say, I want to speak to the Wizard. A moment later he would pass around the telephone, and coming out of the receiver there would be a voice, a man's voice, saying over and over: five of hearts, five of hearts, five of hearts. Then he would thank the Wizard, hang up the phone, and stand there grinning at everyone.

Years later, when it was finally explained to A., it all seemed so simple. His grandfather and a friend had each agreed to be the Wizard for the other. The question, May I speak to the Wizard, was a signal, and the man on the other end of the line would start reeling off the suits: spade, heart, diamond, club. When he hit the right one, the caller would say something, anything, meaning go no further, and then the Wizard would go through the litany of numbers: ace, two, three, four, five, etc. When he came to the right one, the caller would again say something, and the Wizard would stop, put the two elements together, and repeat them into the phone: five of hearts, five of hearts, five of hearts.

The Book of Memory. Book Six.

He finds it extraordinary, even in the ordinary actuality of his experience, to feel his feet on the ground, to feel his lungs expanding and contracting with the air he breathes, to know that if he puts one foot in front of the other he will be able to walk from where he is to where he is going. He finds it extraordinary that on some mornings, just after he has woken up, as he bends down to tie his shoes, he is flooded with a happiness so intense, a happiness so naturally and harmoniously at one with the world, that he can feel himself alive in the present, a present that surrounds him and permeates him, that breaks through him with the sudden, overwhelming knowledge that he is alive. And the happiness he discovers in himself at that moment is extraordinary. And whether or not it is extraordinary, he finds this happiness extraordinary.

Sometimes it feels as though we are wandering through a city without purpose. We walk down the street, turn at random down another street, stop to admire the cornice of a building,

bend down to inspect a splotch of tar on the pavement that re-
minds us of certain paintings we have admired, look at the faces
of the people who pass us on the street, trying to imagine the
lives they carry around inside them, go into a cheap restaurant
for lunch, walk back outside and continue on our way toward
the river (if this city has a river), to watch the boats as they sail
by, or the big ships docked in the harbor, perhaps singing to ourselves as we walk, or perhaps whistling, or perhaps trying to remember something we have forgotten. Sometimes it seems as
though we are not going anywhere as we walk through the city,
that we are only looking for a way to pass the time, and that it is
only our fatigue that tells us where and when we should stop.
But just as one step will inevitably lead to the next step, so it is
that one thought inevitably follows from the previous thought,
and in the event that a thought should engender more than a single thought (say two or three thoughts, equal to each other in all
their consequences), it will be necessary not only to follow the
first thought to its conclusion, but also to backtrack to the original position of that thought in order to follow the second
thought to its conclusion, and then the third thought, and so on,
and in this way, if we were to try to make an image of this process in our minds, a network of paths begins to be drawn, as in
the image of the human bloodstream (heart, arteries, veins, cap-
illaries), or as in the image of a map (of city streets, for example,
preferably a large city, or even of roads, as in the gas station
maps of roads that stretch, bisect, and meander across a conti-
nent), so that what we are really doing when we walk through
the city is thinking, and thinking in such a way that our thoughts
compose a journey, and this journey is no more or less than the
steps we have taken, so that, in the end, we might safely say that
we have been on a journey, and even if we do not leave our
room, it has been a journey, and we might safely say that we
have been somewhere, even if we don't know where it is.

He takes down from his bookshelf a brochure he bought ten
years ago in Amherst, Massachusetts, a souvenir of his visit to
Emily Dickinson's house, thinking now of the strange exhaustion that had afflicted him that day as he stood in the poet's

room: a shortness of breath, as if he had just climbed to the top of a mountain. He had walked around that small, sun-drenched room, looking at the white bedspread, the polished furniture, thinking of the seventeen hundred poems that were written there, trying to see them as a part of those four walls, and yet failing to do so. For if words are a way of being in the world, he thought, then even if there were no world to enter, the world was already there, in that room, which meant it was the room that was present in the poems and not the reverse. He reads now, on the last page of the brochure, in the awkward prose of the anonymous writer:

"In this bedroom-workroom, Emily announced that the soul could be content with its own society. But she discovered that consciousness was captivity as well as liberty, so that even here she was prey to her own self-imprisonment in despair or fear. . . . For the sensitive visitor, then, Emily's room acquires an atmosphere encompassing the poet's several moods of superiority, anxiety, anguish, resignation or ecstasy. Perhaps more than any other concrete place in American literature, it symbolizes a native tradition, epitomized by Emily, of an assiduous study of the inner life."

Song to accompany The Book of Memory. *Solitude*, as sung by Billie Holiday. In the recording of May 9, 1941 by Billie Holiday and Her Orchestra. Performance time: three minutes and fifteen seconds. As follows: In my solitude you haunt me / With reveries of days gone by. / In my solitude you taunt me / With memories that never die . . . Etc. With credits to D. Ellington, E. De Lange, and I. Mills.

First allusions to a woman's voice. To be followed by specific reference to several.

For it is his belief that if there is a voice of truth—assuming there is such a thing as truth, and assuming this truth can speak—it comes from the mouth of a woman.

It is also true that memory sometimes comes to him as a voice. It is a voice that speaks inside him, and it is not necessarily his

own. It speaks to him in the way a voice might tell stories to a
child, and yet at times this voice makes fun of him, or calls him
to attention, or curses him in no uncertain terms. At times it
willfully distorts the story it is telling him, changing facts to
suit its whims, catering to the interests of drama rather than
truth. Then he must speak to it in his own voice and tell it to
stop, thus returning it to the silence it came from. At other
times it sings to him. At still other times it whispers. And then
there are the times it merely hums, or babbles, or cries out in
pain. And even when it says nothing, he knows it is still there,
and in the silence of this voice that says nothing, he waits for it
to speak.

Jeremiah: "Then said I, Ah, Lord God! behold, I cannot speak:
for I am a child. But the Lord said unto me, say not, I am a
child: for thou shalt go to all that I shall send thee, and whatsoever I command thee thou shalt speak. . . . Then the Lord put
forth his hand, and touched my mouth. And the Lord said unto
me, Behold, I have put my words in thy mouth."

The Book of Memory. Book Seven.
    First commentary on the Book of Jonah.
    One is immediately struck by its oddness in relation to the
other prophetic books. This brief work, the only one to be written in the third person, is more dramatically a story of solitude
than anything else in the Bible, and yet it is told as if from outside that solitude, as if, by plunging into the darkness of that
solitude, the "I" has vanished from itself. It cannot speak about
itself, therefore, except as another. As in Rimbaud's phrase: "Je
est un autre."
    Not only is Jonah reluctant to speak (as Jeremiah is, for ex-
ample), but he actually refuses to speak. "Now the word of the
Lord came unto Jonah. . . . But Jonah rose up to flee from the
presence of the Lord."
    Jonah flees. He books passage aboard a ship. A terrible
storm rises up, and the sailors fear they will drown. Everyone
prays for deliverance. But Jonah has "gone down into the sides
of the ship; and he lay, and was fast asleep." Sleep, then, as the

ultimate withdrawal from the world. Sleep as an image of solitude. Oblomov curled on his couch, dreaming himself back
into his mother's womb. Jonah in the belly of the ship; Jonah
in the belly of the whale.

The captain of the ship finds Jonah and tells him to pray to
his God. Meanwhile, the sailors have drawn lots, to see which
among them has been responsible for the storm, ". . . and the
lot fell upon Jonah.

"And then he said unto them, Take me up, and cast me forth
into the sea; so shall the sea be calm unto you; for I know that
for my sake this great tempest is upon you.

"Nevertheless the men rowed hard to bring it to the land; but
they could not; for the sea wrought, and was tempestuous
against them. . . .

"So they took up Jonah, and cast him forth into the sea; and
the sea ceased from her raging."

The popular mythology about the whale notwithstanding,
the great fish that swallows Jonah is by no means an agent of
destruction. The fish is what saves him from drowning in the
sea. "The waters compassed me about, even to the soul: the
depth closed me round about, the weeds were wrapped about
my head." In the depth of that solitude, which is equally the
depth of silence, as if in the refusal to speak there were an equal
refusal to turn one's face to the other ("Jonah rose up to flee
from the presence of the Lord")—which is to say: who seeks
solitude seeks silence; who does not speak is alone; is alone,
even unto death—Jonah encounters the darkness of death. We
are told that "Jonah was in the belly of the fish three days and
three nights," and elsewhere, in a chapter of the *Zohar*, we are
told," 'Three days and three nights': which means the three
days that a man is in his grave before his belly bursts apart."
And when the fish then vomits Jonah onto dry land, Jonah is
given back to life, as if the death he had found in the belly of the
fish were a preparation for new life, a life that has passed
through death, and therefore a life that can at last speak. For
death has frightened him into opening his mouth. "I cried by
reason of mine affliction unto the Lord, and he heard me; out of
the belly of hell cried I, and thou heardest my voice." In the

darkness of the solitude that is death, the tongue is finally loosened, and at the moment it begins to speak, there is an answer. And even if there is no answer, the man has begun to speak.

The prophet. As in false: speaking oneself into the future, not by knowledge but by intuition. The real prophet knows. The false prophet guesses.

This was Jonah's greatest problem. If he spoke God's message, telling the Ninevites they would be destroyed in forty days for their wickedness, he was certain they would repent, and thus be spared. For he knew that God was "merciful, slow to anger, and of great kindness."

"So the people of Ninevah believed God, and proclaimed a fast, and put on sackcloth, from the greatest of them even to the least of them."

And if the Ninevites were spared, would this not make Jonah's prophecy false? Would he not, then, be a false prophet? Hence the paradox at the heart of the book: the prophecy would remain true only if he did not speak it. But then, of course, there would be no prophecy, and Jonah would no longer be a prophet. But better to be no prophet at all than to be a false prophet. "Therefore now, O lord, take, I beseech thee, my life from me; for it is better for me to die than to live."

Therefore, Jonah held his tongue. Therefore, Jonah ran away from the presence of the Lord and met the doom of shipwreck. That is to say, the shipwreck of the singular.

Remission of cause and effect.

A. remembers a moment from boyhood (twelve, thirteen years old). He was wandering aimlessly one November afternoon with his friend D. Nothing was happening. But in each of them, at that moment, a sense of infinite possibilities. Nothing was happening. Or else one could say that it was this consciousness of possibility, in fact, that was happening.

As they walked along through the cold, gray air of that afternoon, A. suddenly stopped and announced to his friend: One year from today something extraordinary will happen to us, something that will change our lives forever.

The year passed, and on the appointed day nothing extraordinary happened. A. explained to D.: No matter; the important thing will happen next year. When the second year rolled around, the same thing happened: nothing. But A. and D. were undaunted. All through the years of high school, they continued to commemorate that day. Not with ceremony, but simply with acknowledgement. For example, seeing each other in the school corridor and saying: Saturday is the day. It was not that they still expected a miracle to happen. But, more curiously, over the years they had both become attached to the memory of their prediction.

The reckless future, the mystery of what has not yet happened: this, too, he learned, can be preserved in memory. And it sometimes strikes him that the blind, adolescent prophecy he made twenty years ago, that fore-seeing of the extraordinary, was in fact the extraordinary thing itself: his mind leaping happily into the unknown. For the fact of the matter is, many years have passed. And still, at the end of each November, he finds himself remembering that day.

Prophecy. As in true. As in Cassandra, speaking from the solitude of her cell. As in a woman's voice.

The future falls from her lips in the present, each thing exactly as it will happen, and it is her fate never to be believed. Madwoman, the daughter of Priam: "the shrieks of that ill-omened bird" from whom ". . . sounds of woe / Burst dreadful, as she chewed the laurel leaf, / And ever and anon, like the black Sphinx, / Poured the full tide of enigmatic song." (Lycophron's *Cassandra;* in Royston's translation, 1806). To speak of the future is to use a language that is forever ahead of itself, consigning things that have not yet happened to the past, to an "already" that is forever behind itself, and in this space between utterance and act, word after word, a chasm begins to open, and for one to contemplate such emptiness for any length of time is to grow dizzy, to feel oneself falling into the abyss.

A. remembers the excitement he felt in Paris in 1974, when he discovered the seventeen-hundred line poem by Lycophron (circa 300 B.C.), which is a monologue of Cassandra's ravings in prison before the fall of Troy. He came to the poem through a translation into French by Q., a writer just his own age (twenty-four). Three years later, when he got together with Q. in a cafe on the rue Condé, he asked him whether he knew of any translations of the poem into English. Q. himself did not read or speak English, but yes, he had heard of one, by a certain Lord Royston at the beginning of the nineteenth century. When A. returned to New York in the summer of 1974, he went to the Columbia University library to look for the book. Much to his surprise, he found it. *Cassandra, translated from the original Greek of Lycophron and illustrated with notes;* Cambridge, 1806.

This translation was the only work of any substance to come from the pen of Lord Royston. He had completed the translation while still an undergraduate at Cambridge and had published the poem himself in a luxurious private edition. Then he had gone on the traditional continental tour following his graduation. Because of the Napoleonic tumult in France, he did not head south—which would have been the natural route for a young man of his interests—but instead went north, to the Scandinavian countries, and in 1808, while traveling through the treacherous waters of the Baltic Sea, drowned in a shipwreck off the coast of Russia. He was just twenty-four years old.

Lycophron: "the obscure." In his dense, bewildering poem, nothing is ever named, everything becomes a reference to something else. One is quickly lost in the labyrinth of its associations, and yet one continues to run through it, propelled by the force of Cassandra's voice. The poem is a verbal outpouring, breathing fire, consumed by fire, which obliterates itself at the edge of sense. "Cassandra's word," as a friend of A.'s put it (B.: in a lecture, curiously enough, about Hölderlin's poetry—a poetry which he compares in manner to Cassandra's speech), "this irreducible sign—*deutungslos*—a word beyond grasping, Cassandra's word, a word from which no lesson is to be drawn, a word, each time, and every time, spoken to say nothing. . . ."

After reading through Royston's translation, A. realized that a great talent had been lost in that shipwreck. Royston's English rolls along with such fury, such deft and acrobatic syntax, that to read the poem is to feel yourself trapped inside Cassandra's mouth.

line 240   An oath! they have an oath in heaven!
Soon shall their sail be spread, and in their hands
The strong oar quivering cleave the refluent wave;
While songs, and hymns, and carols jubilant
Shall charm the rosy God, to whom shall rise,
Rife from Apollo's Delphic shrine, the smoke
Of numerous holocausts: Well pleased shall hear
Enorches, where the high-hung taper's light
Gleams on his dread carousals, and when forth
The Savage rushes on the corny field
Mad to destroy, shall bid his vines entwist
His sinewy strength, and hurl them to the ground.

*

line 426   ... then Greece
For this one crime, aye for this one, shall weep
Myriads of sons: no funeral urn, but rocks
Shall hearse their bones; no friends upon their dust
Shall pour the dark libations of the dead;
A name, a breath, an empty sound remains,
A fruitless marble warm with bitter tears
Of sires, and orphan babes, and widowed wives!

*

line 1686   Why pour the fruitless strain? to winds, and waves,
Deaf winds, dull waves, and senseless shades of woods
I chaunt, and sing mine unavailing song.
Such woes has Lepsieus heaped upon my head,
Steeping my words in incredulity;
The jealous God! for from my virgin couch
I drove him amorous, nor returned his love.
But fate is in my voice, truth on my lips;
What must come, will come; and when rising woes
Burst on his head, when rushing from her seat
His country falls, nor man nor God can save,

Some wretch shall groan, "From her no falsehood
flowed,
True were the shrieks of that ill-omened bird."

It intrigues A. to consider that both Royston and Q. had
translated this work while still in their early twenties. In spite of
the century and a half that separated them, each had given some
special force to his own language through the medium of this
poem. At one point, it occurred to him that perhaps Q. was a
reincarnation of Royston. Every hundred years or so Royston
would be reborn to translate the poem into another language,
and just as Cassandra was destined never to be believed, the
work of Lycophron would remain unread, generation after generation. A useless task therefore: to write a book that would stay
forever closed. And still, the image rises up in his mind: shipwreck. Consciousness falling to the bottom of the sea, and the
horrible noise of cracking wood, the tall masts tumbling into the
waves. To imagine Royston's thoughts the moment his body
smacked against the water. To imagine the havoc of that death.

The Book of Memory. Book Eight.
By the time of his third birthday, A.'s son's taste in literature
had begun to expand from simple, heavily illustrated baby
books to more sophisticated children's books. The illustration
was still a source of great pleasure, but it was no longer crucial.
The story itself had become enough to hold his attention, and
when A. came to a page with no picture at all, he would be
moved to see the little boy looking intently ahead, at nothing, at
the emptiness of the air, at the blank wall, imagining what the
words were telling him. "It's fun to imagine that we can't see,"
he told his father once, as they were walking down the street.
Another time, the boy went into the bathroom, closed the door,
and did not come out. A. asked through the closed door: "What
are you doing in there?" "I'm thinking," the boy said. "I have
to be alone to think."

Little by little, they both began to gravitate toward one book.
The story of Pinocchio. First in the Disney version, and then,

soon after, in the original version, with text by Collodi and illustrations by Mussino. The little boy never tired of hearing the
chapter about the storm at sea, which tells of how Pinocchio
finds Gepetto in the belly of the Terrible Shark.

"Oh, Father, dear Father! Have I found you at last? Now I
shall never, never leave you again!"

Gepetto explains: "The sea was rough and the whitecaps
overturned the boat. Then a Terrible Shark came up out of the
sea and, as soon as he saw me in the water, swam quickly toward me, put out his tongue, and swallowed me as easily as if I
had been a chocolate peppermint."

"And how long have you been shut away in here?"

"From that day to this, two long weary years—two years, my
Pinocchio. . . ."

"And how have you lived? Where did you find the candle?
And the matches to light it with—where did you get them?"

"In the storm which swamped my boat, a large ship also suffered the same fate. The sailors were all saved, but the ship
went right down to the bottom of the sea, and the same Terrible
Shark that swallowed me, swallowed most of it. . . . To my
own good luck, that ship was loaded with meat, preserved
foods, crackers, bread, bottles of wine, raisins, cheese, coffee,
sugar, wax candles, and boxes of matches. With all these bless-
ings, I have been able to live on for two whole years, but now I
am at the very last crumbs. Today there is nothing left in the
cupboard, and this candle you see here is the last one I have."

"And then?"

"And then, my dear, we'll find ourselves in darkness."

For A. and his son, so often separated from each other during the past year, there was something deeply satisfying in this
passage of reunion. In effect, Pinocchio and Gepetto are separated throughout the entire book. Gepetto is given the mysterious piece of talking wood by the carpenter, Master Cherry,
in the second chapter. In the third chapter the old man sculpts
the Marionette. Even before Pinocchio is finished, his pranks
and mischief begin. "I deserve it," says Gepetto to himself.
"I should have thought of this before I made him. Now it's too
late." At this point, like any newborn baby, Pinocchio is pure

will, libidinous need without consciousness. Very rapidly, over the next few pages, Gepetto teaches his son to walk, the Marionette experiences hunger and accidentally burns his feet off—which his father rebuilds for him. The next day Gepetto sells his coat to buy Pinocchio an A-B-C book for school ("Pinocchio understood . . . and, unable to restrain his tears, he jumped on his father's neck and kissed him over and over"), and then, for more than two hundred pages, they do not see each other again. The rest of the book tells the story of Pinocchio's search for his father—and Gepetto's search for his son. At some point, Pinocchio realizes that he wants to become a real boy. But it also becomes clear that this will not happen until he is reunited with his father. Adventures, misadventures, detours, new resolves, struggles, happenstance, progress, setbacks, and through it all, the gradual dawning of conscience. The superiority of the Collodi original to the Disney adaptation lies in its reluctance to make the inner motivations of the story explicit. They remain intact, in a pre-conscious, dream-like form, whereas in Disney these things are expressed—which sentimentalizes them, and therefore trivializes them. In Disney, Gepetto prays for a son; in Collodi, he simply makes him. The physical act of shaping the puppet (from a piece of wood that talks, that is *alive*, which mirrors Michaelangelo's notion of sculpture: the figure is already there in the material; the artist merely hews away at the excess matter until the true form is revealed, implying that Pinocchio's being precedes his body: his task throughout the book is to find it, in other words to find himself, which means that this is a story of becoming rather than of birth), this act of shaping the puppet is enough to convey the idea of the prayer, and surely it is more powerful for remaining silent. Likewise with Pinocchio's efforts to attain real boyhood. In Disney, he is commanded by the Blue Fairy to be "brave, truthful, and unselfish," as though there were an easy formula for taking hold of the self. In Collodi, there are no directives. Pinocchio simply blunders about, simply lives, and little by little comes to an awareness of what he can become. The only improvement Disney makes on the story, and this is perhaps arguable, comes at the end, in the episode of the escape from the Terrible Shark (Monstro the Whale). In Collodi, the Shark's mouth is open (he suffers from asthma and heart disease), and to organize the escape Pinocchio needs no more than courage. "Then, my dear Father, there is no time to lose. We must escape."

"Escape! How?"

"We can run out of the Shark's mouth and dive into the sea."

"You speak well, but I cannot swim, my dear Pinocchio."

"Why should that matter? You can climb on my shoulders and I, who am a fine swimmer, will carry you safely to shore."

"Dreams, my boy!" answered Gepetto, shaking his head and smiling sadly. "Do you think it possible for a Marionette, a yard high, to have the strength to carry me on his shoulders and swim?"

"Try it and see! And in any case, if it is written that we must die, we shall at least die together." Not adding another word, Pinocchio took the candle in his hand and going ahead to light the way, he said to his father: "Follow me and have no fear."

In Disney, however, Pinocchio needs resourcefulness as well. The whale's mouth is shut, and when it opens, it is only to let water in, not out. Pinocchio cleverly decides to build a fire inside the whale—which induces Monstro to sneeze, thereby launching the puppet and his father into the sea. But more is lost with this flourish than gained. For the crucial image of the story is eliminated: Pinocchio swimming through the desolate water, nearly sinking under the weight of Gepetto's body, making his way through the gray-blue night (page 296 of the American edition), with the moon shining above them, a benign smile on its face, and the huge open mouth of the shark behind them. The father on his son's back: the image evoked here is so clearly that of Aeneas bearing Anchises on his back from the ruins of Troy that each time A. reads the story aloud to his son, he cannot help seeing (for it is not thinking, really, so quickly do these things happen in his mind) certain clusters of other images, spinning outward from the core of his preoccupations: Cassandra, for example, predicting the ruin of Troy, and thereafter loss, as in the wanderings of Aeneas that precede the founding of Rome, and in that wandering the image of another wandering: the Jews in the desert, which, in its turn, yields further clusters of images: "Next year in Jerusalem," and with it the photograph in the Jewish Encyclopedia of his relative, who bore the name of his son.

A. has watched his son's face carefully during these readings of *Pinocchio*. He has concluded that it is the image of Pinocchio saving Gepetto (swimming away with the old man on his back) that gives the story meaning for him. A boy of three is indeed very little. A wisp of puniness against the bulk of his father, he dreams of acquiring inordinate powers to conquer the paltry reality of himself. He is still too young to understand that one day he will be as big as his father, and even when it is explained to him very carefully, the facts are still open to gross misinterpretations: "And some day I'll be the same tall as you, and you'll be the same little as me." The fascination with comic book super-heroes is perhaps understandable from this point of view. It is the dream of being big, of becoming an adult. "What does Superman do?" "He saves people." For this act of saving is in effect what a father does: he saves his little boy from harm. And for the little boy to see Pinocchio, that same foolish puppet who has stumbled his way from one misfortune to the next, who has wanted to be "good" and could not help being "bad," for this same incompetent little marionette, who is not even a real boy, to become a figure of redemption, the very being who saves his father from the grip of death, is a sublime moment of revelation. The son saves the father. This must be fully imagined from the perspective of the little boy. And this, in the mind of the father who was once a little boy, a son, that is, to his own father, must be fully imagined. *Puer aeternus.* The son saves the father.

Further commentary on the nature of chance.

He does not want to neglect to mention that two years after meeting S. in Paris, he happened to meet S.'s younger son on a subsequent visit—through channels and circumstances that had nothing to do with S. himself. This young man, P., who was precisely the same age as A., was working his way to a position of considerable power with an important French film producer. A. himself would later work for this same producer, doing a variety of odd jobs for him in 1971 and 1972 (translating, ghost writing), but none of that is essential. What matters is that by the mid to late seventies, P. had managed to achieve the status of co-producer, and along with the son of the French producer put together the movie *Superman*, which had cost so many millions of dollars, A. read, that it had been described as the most expensive work of art in the history of the Western world.

Early in the summer of 1980, shortly after his son turned three, A. and the boy spent a week together in the country, in a house owned by friends who were off on vacation. A. noticed in the newspaper that *Superman* was playing in a local theater and decided to take the boy, on the off-chance that he would be able to sit through it. For the first half of the film, the boy was calm, working his way through a bin of popcorn, whispering his questions as A. had instructed him to do, and taking the business of exploding planets, rocket ships, and outer space without much fuss. But then something happened. Superman began to fly, and all at once the boy lost his composure. His mouth dropped open, he stood up in his seat, spilled his popcorn, pointed at the screen, and began to shout: "Look! Look! He's flying!" For the rest of the film, he was beside himself, his face taut with fear and fascination, rattling off questions to his father, trying to absorb what he had seen, marveling, trying to absorb it again, marveling. Toward the end, it became a little too much for him. "Too much booming," he said. His father asked him if he wanted to leave, and he said yes. A. picked him up and carried him out of the theater—into a violent hail storm. As they ran toward the car, the boy said (bouncing up and down in A.'s arms), "We're having quite an adventure tonight, aren't we?"

For the rest of the summer, Superman was his passion, his obsession, the unifying purpose of his life. He refused to wear any shirt except the blue one with the S on the front. His mother sewed a cape together for him, and each time he went outside, he insisted on wearing it, charging down the streets with his arms in front of him, as if flying, stopping only to announce to each passerby under the age of ten: "I'm Superman!" A. was amused by all this, since he could remember these same

things from his own childhood. It was not this obsession that
struck him; nor even, finally, the coincidence of knowing the
men who had made the film that led to this obsession. Rather, it
was this. Each time he saw his son pretending to be Superman,
he could not help thinking of his friend S., as if even the S on his
son's T-shirt were not a reference to Superman but to his friend.
And he wondered at this trick his mind continued to play on
him, this constant turning of one thing into another thing, as if
behind each real thing there were a shadow thing, as alive in his
mind as the thing before his eyes, and in the end he was at a loss
to say which of these things he was actually seeing. And therefore it happened, often it happened, that his life no longer
seemed to dwell in the present.

The Book of Memory. Book Nine.

For most of his adult life, he has earned his living by translating
the books of other writers. He sits at his desk reading the book in
French and then picks up his pen and writes the same book in English. It is both the same book and not the same book, and the
strangeness of this activity has never failed to impress him. Every
book is an image of solitude. It is a tangible object that one can
pick up, put down, open, and close, and its words represent many
months, if not many years, of one man's solitude, so that with
each word one reads in a book one might say to himself that he is
confronting a particle of that solitude. A man sits alone in a room
and writes. Whether the book speaks of loneliness or companionship, it is necessarily a product of solitude. A. sits down in his
own room to translate another man's book, and it is as though he
were entering that man's solitude and making it his own. But
surely that is impossible. For once a solitude has been breached,
once a solitude has been taken on by another, it is no longer solitude, but a kind of companionship. Even though there is only one
man in the room, there are two. A. imagines himself as a kind of
ghost of that other man, who is both there and not there, and
whose book is both the same and not the same as the one he is
translating. Therefore, he tells himself, it is possible to be alone
and not alone at the same moment.

A word becomes another word, a thing becomes another

thing. In this way, he tells himself, it works in the same way that memory does. He imagines an immense Babel inside him. There is a text, and it translates itself into an infinite number of languages. Sentences spill out of him at the speed of thought, and each word comes from a different language, a thousand tongues that clamor inside him at once, the din of it echoing through a maze of rooms, corridors, and stairways, hundreds of stories high. He repeats. In the space of memory, everything is both itself and something else. And then it dawns on him that everything he is trying to record in The Book of Memory, everything he has written so far, is no more than the translation of a moment or two of his life—those moments he lived through on Christmas Eve, 1979, in his room at 6 Varick Street.

The moment of illumination that burns across the sky of solitude.

Pascal in his room on the night of November 23, 1654, sewing the Memorial into the lining of his clothes, so that at any moment, for the rest of his life, he could find beneath his hand the record of that ecstasy.

In the Year of Grace 1654
On Monday, November 23rd, Feast of Saint Clement,
Pope and Martyr,
and of others in the Martyrology.
and eve of Saint Chrysogomus and other Martyrs.
From about half past ten at night until about half past twelve.

Fire
"God of Abraham, God of Isaac, God of Jacob,"
not of the philosophers and scientists.
Certainty. Certainty. Feeling. Joy. Peace.

• • •

Greatness of the human soul.

• • •

Joy, joy, joy, tears of joy.

• • •

I will not forget thy word. Amen.

• • •

Concerning the power of memory.

In the spring of 1966, not long after meeting his future wife, A. was invited by her father (an English professor at Columbia) to the family apartment on Morningside Drive for dessert and coffee. The dinner guests were Francis Ponge and his wife, and A.'s future father-in-law thought that the young A. (just nineteen at the time), would enjoy meeting so famous a writer. Ponge, the master poet of the object, who had invented a poetry more firmly placed in the outer world perhaps than any other, was teaching a course at Columbia that semester. By then A. already spoke reasonably good French. Since Ponge and his wife spoke no English, and A.'s future in-laws spoke almost no French, A. joined in the discussion more fully than he might have, given his innate shyness and penchant for saying nothing whenever possible. He remembers Ponge as a gracious and lively man with sparkling blue eyes.

The second time A. met Ponge was in 1969 (although it could have been 1968 or 1970) at a party given in Ponge's honor by G., a Barnard professor who had been translating his work. When A. shook Ponge's hand, he introduced himself by saying that although he probably didn't remember it, they had once met in New York several years ago. On the contrary, Ponge replied, he remembered the evening quite well. And then he proceeded to talk about the apartment in which that dinner had taken place, describing it in all its details, from the view out the windows to the color of the couch and the arrangement of the furniture in each of the various rooms. For a man to remember so precisely things he had seen only once, things which could not have had any bearing on his life except for a fleeting instant, struck A. with all the force of a supernatural act. He realized that for Ponge there was no division between the work of writing and the work of seeing. For no word can be written without first having been seen, and before it finds its way to the page it must first have been part of the body, a physical presence that one has lived with in the same way one lives with one's heart, one's stomach, and one's brain. Memory, then, not so much as the past contained within us, but as proof of our life in the present. If a man is to be truly present among his surroundings, he must be thinking not of himself, but of what he sees. He must forget himself in order to be there. And from that forgetfulness arises the power of memory. It is a way of living one's life so that nothing is ever lost.

It is also true that "the man with a good memory does not remember anything because he does not forget anything," as Beckett has written about Proust. And it is true that one must make a distinction between voluntary and involuntary memory, as Proust does during the course of his long novel about the past.

What A. feels he is doing, however, as he writes the pages of his own book, is something that does not belong to either one of these two types of memory. A. has both a good memory and a bad memory. He has lost much, but he has also retained much. As he writes, he feels that he is moving inward (through himself) and at the same time moving outward (toward the world). What he experienced, perhaps, during those few moments on Christmas Eve, 1979, as he sat alone in his room on Varick Street, was this: the sudden knowledge that came over him that even alone, in the deepest solitude of his room, he was not alone, or, more precisely, that the moment he began to try to speak of that solitude, he had become more than just himself. Memory, therefore, not simply as the resurrection of one's private past, but an immersion in the past of others, which is to say: history—which one both participates in and is a witness to, is a part of and apart from. Everything, therefore, is present in his mind at once, as if each element were reflecting the light of all the others, and at the same time emitting its own unique and unquenchable radiance. If there is any reason for him to be in this room now, it is because there is something inside him hungering to see it all at once, to savor the chaos of it in all its raw and urgent simultaneity. And yet, the telling of it is necessarily slow, a delicate business of trying to remember what has already been remembered. The pen will never be able to move fast enough to write down every word discovered in the space of memory. Some things have been lost forever, other things will perhaps be remembered again, and still other things have been lost and found and lost again. There is no way to be sure of any of this.

Possible epigraph(s) for The Book of Memory.

"Thoughts come at random, and go at random. No device for holding on to them or for having them. A thought has escaped: I was trying to write it down: instead I write that it has escaped me." (Pascal)

"As I write down my thought, it sometimes escapes me; but this makes me remember my own weakness, which I am constantly forgetting. This teaches me as much as my forgotten thought, for I strive only to know my own nothingness." (Pascal)

The Book of Memory. Book Ten.

When he speaks of the room, he does not mean to neglect the windows that are sometimes present in the room. The room need not be an image of hermetic consciousness, and when a man or a woman stands or sits alone in a room there is more that happens there, he realizes, than the silence of thought, the silence of a body struggling to put its thoughts into words. Nor does he mean to imply that only suffering takes place within the four walls of consciousness, as in the allusions made to Hölderlin and Emily Dickinson previously. He thinks, for example, of Vermeer's women, alone in their rooms, with the bright light of the real world pouring through a window, either open or closed, and the utter stillness of those solitudes, an almost heartbreaking evocation of the everyday and its domestic variables. He thinks, in particular, of a painting he saw on his trip to Amsterdam, *Woman in Blue*, which nearly immobilized him with contemplation in the Rijksmuseum. As one commentator has written:

"The letter, the map, the woman's pregnancy, the empty chair, the open box, the unseen window—all are reminders or natural emblems of absence, of the unseen, of other minds, wills, times, and places, of past and future, of birth and perhaps of death—in general, of a world that extends beyond the edges of the frame, and of larger, wider horizons that encompass and impinge upon the scene suspended before our eyes. And yet it is the fullness and self-sufficiency of the present moment that Vermeer insists upon—with such conviction that its capacity to orient and contain is invested with metaphysical value."

Even more than the objects mentioned in this list, it is the quality of the light coming through the unseen window to the viewer's left that so warmly beckons him to turn his attention to the outside, to the world beyond the painting. A. stares hard at the woman's face, and as time passes he almost begins to hear the voice inside the woman's head as she reads the letter in her hands. She, so very pregnant, so tranquil in the immanence of motherhood, with the letter taken out of the box, no doubt being read for the hundredth time; and there, hanging on the wall to her right, a map of the world, which is the image of everything that exists outside the room: that light, pouring gently over her face and shining on her blue smock, the belly bulging with life, and its blueness bathed in luminosity, a light so pale it verges on whiteness. To follow with more of the same: *Woman Pouring Milk, Woman Holding a Balance, Woman Putting on Pearls, Young Woman at a Window with a Pitcher, Girl Reading a Letter at an Open Window.*

"The fullness and self-sufficiency of the present moment."

If it was Rembrandt and Titus who in some sense lured A. to Amsterdam, where he then entered rooms and found himself in the presence of women (Vermeer's women, Anne Frank), his trip to that city was at the same time conceived as a pilgrimage to his own past. Again, his inner movements were expressed in the form of paintings: an emotional state finding tangible representation in a work of art, as though another's solitude were in fact the echo of his own.

In this case it was Van Gogh, and the new museum that had

been built to house his work. Like some early trauma buried in the unconscious, forever linking two unrelated objects (this shoe is my father; this rose is my mother), Van Gogh's paintings stand in his mind as an image of his adolescence, a translation of his deepest feelings of that period. He can even be quite precise about it, pinpointing events and his reactions to events by place and time (exact locations, exact moments: year, month, day, even hour and minute). What matters, however, is not so much the sequence of the chronicle as its consequences, its permanence in the space of memory. To remember, therefore, a day in April when he was sixteen, and cutting school with the girl he had fallen in love with: so passionately and hopelessly that the thought of it still smarts. To remember the train, and then the ferry to New York (that ferry, which has long since vanished: industrial iron, the warm fog, rust), and then going to a large exhibition of Van Gogh paintings. To remember how he had stood there, trembling with happiness, as if the shared seeing of these works had invested them with the girl's presence, had mysteriously varnished them with the love he felt for her.

Some days later, he began writing a sequence of poems (now lost) based on the canvases he had seen, each poem bearing the title of a different Van Gogh painting. These were the first real poems he ever wrote. More than a method for entering those paintings, the poems were an attempt to recapture the memory of that day. Many years went by, however, before he realized this. It was only in Amsterdam, studying the same paintings he had seen with the girl (seeing them for the first time since then—almost half his life ago), that he remembered having written those poems. At that moment the equation became clear to him: the act of writing as an act of memory. For the fact of the matter is, other than the poems themselves, he has not forgotten any of it.

Standing in the Van Gogh Museum in Amsterdam (December 1979) in front of the painting *The Bedroom*, completed in Arles, October 1888.

Van Gogh to his brother: "This time it is just simply my

bedroom . . . To look at the picture ought to rest the brain or rather the imagination . . .

"The walls are pale violet. The floor is of red tiles.

"The wood of the bed and chairs is the yellow of fresh butter, the sheet and pillows very light lemon-green.

"The coverlet scarlet. The window green.

"The toilet table orange, the basin blue.

"The doors lilac.

"And that is all—there is nothing in this room with closed shutters. . . .

"This by way of revenge for the enforced rest I have been obliged to take. . . .

"I will make you sketches of the other rooms too some day."

As A. continued to study the painting, however, he could not help feeling that Van Gogh had done something quite different from what he thought he had set out to do. A.'s first impression was indeed a sense of calm, of "rest," as the artist describes it. But gradually, as he tried to inhabit the room presented on the canvas, he began to experience it as a prison, an impossible space, an image, not so much of a place to live, but of the mind that has been forced to live there. Observe carefully. The bed blocks one door, a chair blocks the other door, the shutters are closed: you can't get in, and once you are in, you can't get out. Stifled among the furniture and everyday objects of the room, you begin to hear a cry of suffering in this painting, and once you hear it, it does not stop. "I cried by reason of mine affliction . . . ." But there is no answer to this cry. The man in this painting (and this is a self-portrait, no different from a picture of a man's face, with eyes, nose, lips, and jaw) has been alone too much, has struggled too much in the depths of solitude. The world ends at that barricaded door. For the room is not a representation of solitude, it is the substance of solitude itself. And it is a thing so heavy, so unbreathable, that it cannot be shown in any terms other than what it is. "And that is all—there is nothing in this room with closed shutters. . . ."

Further commentary on the nature of chance.

A. arrived in London and departed from London, spending a few days on either end of his trip visiting with English friends.

The girl of the ferry and the Van Gogh paintings was English (she had grown up in London, had lived in America from the age of about twelve to eighteen, and had then returned to London to go to art school), and on the first leg of his trip, A. spent several hours with her. Over the years since their graduation from high school, they had kept in touch at best fitfully, had seen each other perhaps five or six times. A. was long cured of his passion, but he had not dismissed her altogether from his mind, clinging somehow to the feeling of that passion, although she herself had lost importance for him. It had been several years since their last meeting, and now he found it gloomy, almost oppressive to be with her. She was still beautiful, he thought, and yet solitude seemed to enclose her, in the same way an egg encloses an unborn bird. She lived alone, had almost no friends. For many years she had been working on sculptures in wood, but she refused to show them to anyone. Each time she finished a piece, she would destroy it, and then begin on the next one. Again, A. had come face to face with a woman's solitude. But here it had turned in on itself and dried up at its source.

A day or two later, he went to Paris, eventually to Amsterdam, and afterwards back to London. He thought to himself: there will be no time to see her again. On one of those days before returning to New York, he was to have dinner with a friend (T., the same friend who had thought they might be cousins) and decided to spend the afternoon at the Royal Academy of Art, where a large exhibition of "Post Impressionist" paintings was on view. The enormous crush of visitors at the museum, however, made him reluctant to stay for the afternoon, as he had planned, and he found himself with three or four extra hours before his dinner appointment. He went to a cheap fish and chips place in Soho for lunch, trying to decide what to do with himself during this free time. He paid up his bill, left the restaurant, turned the corner, and there, as she stood gazing into the display window of a large shoe store, he saw her.

It was not every day that he ran into someone on the London streets (in that city of millions, he knew no more than a few people), and yet this encounter seemed perfectly natural to him, as though it were a commonplace event. He had been thinking about her only a moment before, regretting his decision not to call her, and now that she was there, suddenly standing before his eyes, he could not help feeling that he had willed her to appear.

He walked toward her and spoke her name.

Paintings. Or the collapse of time in images.

In the Royal Academy exhibition he had seen in London, there were several paintings by Maurice Denis. While in Paris, A. had visited the widow of the poet Jean Follain (Follain, who had died in a traffic accident in 1971, just days before A. had moved to Paris) in connection with an anthology of French poetry that A. was preparing, which in fact was what had brought him back to Europe. Madame Follain, he soon learned, was the daughter of Maurice Denis, and many of her father's paintings hung on the walls of the apartment. She herself was now in her late seventies, perhaps eighty, and A. was impressed by her Parisian toughness, her gravel voice, her devotion to her dead husband's work.

One of the paintings in the apartment bore a title: Madelaine à 18 mois (Madelaine at 18 months), which Denis had written out across the top of the canvas. This was the same Madelaine who had grown up to become Follain's wife and who had just asked A. to enter her apartment. For a moment, without being aware of it, she stood in front of that picture, which had been painted nearly eighty years before, and A. saw, as though leaping incredibly across time, that the child's face in the painting and the old woman's face before him were exactly the same. For that one instant, he felt he had cut through the illusion of human time and had experienced it for what it was: as no more than a blink of the eyes. He had seen an entire life standing before him, and it had been collapsed into that one instant.

O. to A. in conversation, describing what it felt like to have become an old man. O., now in his seventies, his memory failing, his face as wrinkled as a half-closed palm. Looking at A. and shaking his head with deadpan wit: "What a strange thing to happen to a little boy."

Yes, it is possible that we do not grow up, that even as we grow old, we remain the children we always were. We remember ourselves as we were then, and we feel ourselves to be the same. We made ourselves into what we are now then, and we remain what we were, in spite of the years. We do not change for ourselves. Time makes us grow old, but we do not change.

The Book of Memory. Book Eleven.

He remembers returning home from his wedding party in 1974, his wife beside him in her white dress, and taking the front door key out of his pocket, inserting the key in the lock, and then, as he turned his wrist, feeling the blade of the key snap off inside the lock.

He remembers that in the spring of 1966, not long after he met his future wife, one of the keys of her piano broke: F above Middle C. That summer the two of them traveled to a remote part of Maine. One day, as they walked through a nearly abandoned town, they wandered into an old meeting hall, which had not been used for years. Remnants of some men's society were scattered about the place: Indian headdresses, lists of names, the detritus of drunken gatherings. The hall was dusty and deserted, except for an upright piano that stood in one corner. His wife began to play (she played well) and discovered that all the keys worked except one: F above Middle C.

It was at that moment, perhaps, that A. realized the world would go on eluding him forever.

If a novelist had used these little incidents of broken piano keys (or the wedding day accident of losing the key inside the door), the reader would be forced to take note, to assume the novelist was trying to make some point about his characters or the world. One could speak of symbolic meanings, of subtext, or simply of formal devices (for as soon as a thing happens more than once, even if it is arbitrary, a pattern takes shape, a form begins to emerge). In a work of fiction, one assumes there is a conscious mind behind the words on the page. In the presence of happenings in the so-called real world, one assumes nothing. The made-up story consists entirely of meanings, whereas the

story of fact is devoid of any significance beyond itself. If a man
says to you, "I'm going to Jerusalem," you think to yourself:
how nice, he's going to Jerusalem. But if a character in a novel
were to speak those same words, "I'm going to Jerusalem,"
your response is not at all the same. You think, to begin with, of
Jerusalem itself: its history, its religious role, its function as a
mythical place. You would think of the past, of the present
(politics; which is also to think of the recent past), and of the
future—as in the phrase: "Next year in Jerusalem." On top of
that, you would integrate these thoughts into whatever it is you
already know about the character who is going to Jerusalem
and use this new synthesis to draw further conclusions, refine
perceptions, think more cogently about the book as a whole.
And then, once the work is finished, the last page read and the
book closed, interpretations begin: psychological, historical,
sociological, structural, philological, religious, sexual, philosophical, either singly or in various combinations, depending on
your bent. Although it is possible to interpret a real life according to any of these systems (people do, after all, go to priests
and psychiatrists; people do sometimes try to understand their
lives in terms of historical conditions), it does not have the same
effect. Something is missing: the grandeur, the grasp of the general, the illusion of metaphysical truth. One says: Don Quixote
is consciousness gone haywire in a realm of the imaginary. One
looks at a mad person in the world (A. at his schizophrenic sister, for example), and says nothing. This is the sadness of a
wasted life, perhaps—but no more.

Now and then, A. finds himself looking at a work of art with
the same eyes he uses to look at the world. To read the imaginary in this way is to destroy it. He thinks, for example, of
Tolstoy's description of the opera in *War and Peace*. Nothing
is taken for granted in this passage, and therefore everything is
reduced to absurdity. Tolstoy makes fun of what he sees simply by describing it. "In the second act there were cardboard
monuments on the stage, and a round hole in the backdrop
representing a moon. Shades had been put over the footlights
and deep notes were played on the horns and contrabass as a
number of people appeared from both sides of the stage wearing

black cloaks and flourishing what looked like daggers. Then some other men ran onto the stage and began dragging away the maiden who had been in white and was now in pale blue. They did not take her away at once, but spent a long time singing with her, until at last they dragged her off, and behind the scenes something metallic was struck three times, and everyone knelt down and sang a prayer. All these actions were repeatedly interrupted by the enthusiastic shouts of the audience."

There is also the equal and opposite temptation to look at the world as though it were an extension of the imaginary. This, too, has sometimes happened to A., but he is loathe to accept it as a valid solution. Like everyone else, he craves a meaning. Like everyone else, his life is so fragmented that each time he sees a connection between two fragments he is tempted to look for a meaning in that connection. The connection exists. But to give it a meaning, to look beyond the bare fact of its existence, would be to build an imaginary world inside the real world, and he knows it would not stand. At his bravest moments, he embraces meaninglessness as the first principle, and then he understands that his obligation is to see what is in front of him (even though it is also inside him) and to say what he sees. He is in his room on Varick Street. His life has no meaning. The book he is writing has no meaning. There is the world, and the things one encounters in the world, and to speak of them is to be in the world. A key breaks off in a lock, and something has happened. That is to say, a key has broken off in a lock. The same piano seems to exist in two different places. A young man, twenty years later, winds up living in the same room where his father faced the horror of solitude. A man encounters his old love on a street in a foreign city. It means only what it is. Nothing more, nothing less. Then he writes: to enter this room is to vanish in a place where past and present meet. And then he writes: as in the phrase: "he wrote The Book of Memory in this room."

The invention of solitude.

He wants to say. That is to say, he means. As in the French, "vouloir dire," which means, literally, to want to say, but

which means, in fact, to mean. He means to say what he wants.
He wants to say what he means. He says what he wants to mean.
He means what he says.

Vienna, 1919.

No meaning, yes. But it would be impossible to say that we
are not haunted. Freud has described such experiences as "uncanny," or *unheimlich*—the opposite of *heimlich*, which means
"familiar," "native," "belonging to the home." The implica-
tion, therefore, is that we are thrust out from the protective
shell of our habitual perceptions, as though we were suddenly
outside ourselves, adrift in a world we do not understand. By
definition, we are lost in that world. We cannot even hope to
find our way in it.

Freud argues that each stage of our development co-exists
with all the others. Even as adults, we have buried within us a
memory of the way we perceived the world as children. And
not simply a memory of it: the structure itself is intact. Freud
connects the experience of the uncanny with a revival of the
egocentric, animistic world-view of childhood. "It would seem
as though each one of us has been through a phase of individual
development corresponding to that animistic stage in primitive
men, that none of us has traversed it without certain traces of it
which can be re-activated, and that everything which now
strikes us as 'uncanny' fulfills the condition of stirring those
vestiges of animistic mental activity within us and bringing
them to expression." He concludes: "An uncanny experience
occurs either when repressed infantile complexes have been revived by some impression, or when the primitive beliefs we
have surmounted seem once more to be confirmed."

None of this, of course, is an explanation. At best it serves to
describe the process, to point out the terrain on which it takes
place. As such, A. is more than willing to accept it as true. Un-
homeness, therefore, as a memory of another, much earlier home
of the mind. In the same way a dream will sometimes resist in-
terpretation until a friend suggests a simple, almost obvious
meaning, A. cannot prove Freud's argument true or false, but it
feels right to him, and he is more than willing to accept it. All

the coincidences that seem to have been multiplying around him, then, are somehow connected with a memory of his childhood, as if by beginning to remember his childhood, the world were returning to a prior state of its being. This feels right to him. He is remembering his childhood, and it has appeared to him in the present in the form of these experiences. He is remembering his childhood, and it is writing itself out for him in the present. Perhaps that is what he means when he writes: "meaninglessness is the first principle." Perhaps that is what he means when he writes: "He means what he says." Perhaps that is what he means. And perhaps it is not. There is no way to be sure of any of this.

The invention of solitude. Or stories of life and death.

The story begins with the end. Speak or die. And for as long as you go on speaking, you will not die. The story begins with death. King Shehriyar has been cuckolded: "and they ceased not from kissing and clipping and clicketing and carousing." He retreats from the world, vowing never to succumb to feminine trickery again. Later, returning to his throne, he gratifies his physical desires by taking in women of the kingdom. Once satisfied, he orders their execution. "And he ceased not to do this for three years, till the land was stripped of marriageable girls, and all the women and mothers and fathers wept and cried out against the King, cursing him and complaining to the Creator of heaven and earth and calling for succor upon Him who heareth prayer and answereth those that cry to Him; and those that had daughters left fled with them, till at last there remained not a single girl in the city apt for marriage."

At this point, Shehrzad, the vizier's daughter, volunteers to go to the King. ("Her memory was stored with verses and stories and folklore and the sayings of Kings and sages, and she was wise, witty, prudent, and well-bred.") Her desperate father tries to dissuade her from going to this sure death, but she is unperturbed. "Marry me to this king, for either I will be the means of the deliverance of the daughters of the Muslims from slaughter, or I will die and perish as others have perished." She goes off to sleep with the king and puts her plan into action:

"to tell . . . delightful stories to pass away the watches of our night . . . ; it shall be the means of my deliverance and the ridding of the folk of this calamity, and by it I will turn the king from his custom."

The king agrees to listen to her. She begins her story, and what she tells is a story about story-telling, a story within which are several stories, each one, in itself, about story-telling—by means of which a man is saved from death.

Day begins to dawn, and mid-way through the first story-within-the-story, Shehrzad falls silent. "This is nothing to what I will tell tomorrow night," she says, "if the king let me live." And the king says to himself, "By Allah, I will not kill her, till I hear the rest of the story." So it goes for three nights, each night's story stopping before the end and spilling over into the beginning of the next night's story, by which time the first cycle of stories has ended and a new one begun. Truly, it is a matter of life and death. On the first night, Shehrzad begins with The Merchant and the Genie. A man stops to eat his lunch in a garden (an oasis in the desert), throws away a date stone, and behold "there started up before him a gigantic spirit, with a naked sword in his hand, who came up to him and said, 'Arise, that I may slay thee, even as thou hast slain my son.' 'How did I slay thy son?' asked the merchant, and the genie replied, 'When thou threwest away the date stone, it smote my son, who was passing at the time, on the breast, and he died forthright.' "

This is guilt out of innocence (echoing the fate of the marriageable girls in the kingdom), and at the same time the birth of enchantment—turning a thought into a thing, bringing the invisible to life. The merchant pleads his case, and the genie agrees to stay his execution. But in exactly one year the merchant must return to the same spot, where the genie will mete out the sentence. Already, a parallel is being drawn with Sherhzad's situation. She wishes to delay her execution, and by planting this idea in the king's mind she is pleading her case—but doing it in such a way that the king cannot recognize it. For this is the function of the story: to make a man see the thing before his eyes by holding up another thing to view.

The year passes, and the merchant, good to his word, returns to the garden. He sits down and begins to weep. An old man wanders by, leading a gazelle by a chain, and asks the merchant what is wrong. The old man is fascinated by what the merchant tells him (as if the merchant's life were a story, with a beginning, middle, and end, a fiction concocted by some other mind—which in fact it is), and decides to wait and see how it will turn out. Then another old man wanders by, leading two black dogs. The conversation is repeated, and then he, too, sits down and waits. Then a third old man wanders by, leading a dappled shemule, and once again the same thing happens. Finally, the genie appears, in a "cloud of dust and a great whirling column from the heart of the desert." Just as he is about to drag off the merchant and slay him with his sword, "as thou slewest my son, the darling of my heart!," the first old man steps forward and says to the genie: "If I relate to thee my history with this gazelle and it seem to thee wonderful, wilt thou grant me a third of this merchant's blood?" Astonishingly, the genie agrees, just as the king has agreed to listen to Sherhzad's story: readily, without a struggle.

Note: the old man does not propose to defend the merchant as one would in a court of law, with arguments, counter-arguments, the presentation of evidence. This would be to make the genie look at the thing he already sees: and about this his mind has been made up. Rather, the old man wishes to turn him away from the facts, turn him away from thoughts of death, and in so doing delight him (literally, "to entice away," from the Latin *delectare*) into a new feeling for life, which in turn will make him renounce his obsession with killing the merchant. An obsession of this sort walls one up in solitude. One sees nothing but one's own thoughts. A story, however, in that it is not a logical argument, breaks down those walls. For it posits the existence of others and allows the listener to come into contact with them—if only in his thoughts.

The old man launches into a preposterous story. This gazelle you see before you, he says, is actually my wife. For thirty years she lived with me and in all that time she could not produce a son. (Again: an allusion to the absent child—the dead child, the child not yet born—referring the genie back to his own sorrow, but obliquely, as part of a world in which life stands equal to death.) "So I took me a concubine and had by her a son like the rising full moon with eyes and eyebrows of perfect beauty. . . ." When the boy was fifteen, the old man went off to another city (he, too, is a merchant), and in his absence the jealous wife used magic to transform the boy and his mother into a calf and a cow. "Thy slave died and her son ran away," the wife told him on his return. After a year of mourning, the cow was slaugh-tered as a sacrifice—through the machinations of the jealous wife. When the man was about to slaughter the calf a moment later, his heart failed him. "And when the calf saw me, he broke his halter and came up to me and fawned on me and moaned and wept, till I took pity on him and said . . . 'Bring me a cow and let this calf go.' " The herdsman's daughter, also learned in the art of magic, later discovered the true identity of the calf. After the merchant granted her the two things she asked for (to marry the son and to bewitch the jealous wife, by imprisoning her in the shape of a beast—"else I shall not be safe from her craft"), she returned the son to his original form. Nor does the story quite end there. The son's bride, the old man goes on to explain, "dwelt with us days and nights and nights and days, till God took her to Himself; and after her death, my son set out on a journey to the land of Ind, which is this merchant's native country; and after a while I took the gazelle and travelled with her from place to place, seeking news of my son, till chance led me to this garden, where I found this merchant sitting weeping; and this is my story." The genie agrees that this is a marvelous story and remits to the old man a third part of the merchant's blood.

One after the other, the two remaining old men propose the same bargain to the genie and begin their stories in the same way. "These two dogs are my elder brothers," says the second old man. "This mule was my wife," says the third. These open-ing sentences contain the essence of the entire project. For what does it mean to look at something, a real object in the real world, an animal, for example, and say that it is something other than what it is? It is to say that each thing leads a double life, at once in the world and in our minds, and that to deny either one of these lives is to kill the thing in both its lives at once. In the stories of the three old men, two mirrors face each other, each one reflecting the light of the other. Both are enchantments, both the real and the imaginary, and each exists by virtue of the other. And it is, truly, a matter of life and death. The first old man has come to the garden in search of his son; the genie has come to the garden to slay his son's unwitting killer. What the old man is telling him is that our sons are always invisible. It is the simplest of truths: a life belongs only to the person who lives it; life itself will claim the living; to live is to let live. And in the end, by means of these three stories, the merchant's life is spared.

This is how *The Thousand and One Nights* begins. At the end of the entire chronicle, after story after story after story, there is a specific result, and it carries with it all the unalterable gravity of a miracle. Sherhzad has borne the king three sons. Again, the lesson is made clear. A voice that speaks, a woman's voice that speaks, a voice that speaks stories of life and death, has the power to give life.

" 'May I then make bold to crave a boon of thy Majesty?'

" 'Ask, O Sherhzad,' answered he, 'and it shall be given unto thee.'

"Whereupon she cried to the nurses and the eunuchs, saying, 'Bring me my children.'

"So they brought them to her in haste, and they were three male children, one walking, one crawling, and one sucking at the breast. She took them and, setting them before the king, kissed the ground and said, 'O King of the age, these are thy children and I crave that thou release me from the doom of death, for the sake of these infants.' "

When the king hears these words, he begins to weep. He gathers the little children up into his arms and declares his love for Sherhzad.

"So they decorated the city in splendid fashion, never before was seen the like thereof, and the drums beat and the pipes sounded, whilst all the mimes and mountebanks and players plied their various arts and the King lavished on them gifts and largesse. Moreover he gave alms to the poor and needy and extended his bounty to all his subjects and the people of his realm."

Mirror text.

If the voice of a woman telling stories has the power to bring children into the world, it is also true that a child has the power to bring stories to life. It is said that a man would go mad if he could not dream at night. In the same way, if a child is not allowed to enter the imaginary, he will never come to grips with the real. A child's need for stories is as fundamental as his need for food, and it manifests itself in the same way hunger does. Tell me a story, the child says. Tell me a story. Tell me a story, daddy, please. The father then sits down and tells a story to his son. Or else he lies down in the dark beside him, the two of them in the child's bed, and begins to speak, as if there were nothing left in the world but his voice, telling a story in the dark to his son. Often it is a fairy tale, or a tale of adventure. Yet often it is no more than a simple leap into the imaginary. Once upon a time there was a little boy named Daniel, A. says to his son named Daniel, and these stories in which the boy himself is the hero are perhaps the most satisfying to him of all. In the same way, A. realizes, as he sits in his room writing The Book of Memory, he speaks of himself as another in order to tell the story of himself. He must make himself absent in order to find himself there. And so he says A., even as he means to say I. For the story of memory is the story of seeing. And even if the things to be seen are no longer there, it is a story of seeing. The voice, therefore, goes on. And even as the boy closes his eyes and goes to sleep, his father's voice goes on speaking in the dark.

The Book of Memory. Book Twelve.

He can go no farther than this. Children have suffered at the hands of adults, for no reason whatsoever. Children have been abandoned, have been left to starve, have been murdered, for no reason whatsoever. It is not possible, he realizes, to go any farther than this.

"But then there are the children," says Ivan Karamazov, "and what am I to do with them?" And again: "I want to forgive. I want to embrace. I don't want any more suffering. And if the sufferings of children go to make up the sum of sufferings which is necessary for the purchase of truth, then I say before-hand that the entire truth is not worth such a price."

Every day, without the least effort, he finds it staring him in the face. These are the days of Cambodia's collapse, and everyday it is there, looking out at him from the newspaper, with the in-evitable photographs of death: the emaciated children, the grownups with nothing left in their eyes. Jim Harrison, for ex-ample, an Oxfam engineer, noting in his diary: "Visited small clinic at kilometer 7. Absolutely no drugs or medicines—serious cases of starvation—clearly just dying for lack of food. . . . The hundreds of children were all marasmic—much skin disease, baldness, discolored hair and great fear in the whole popula-tion." Or later, describing what he saw on a visit to the 7th of January Hospital in Phnom Penh: ". . . terrible conditions—children in bed in filthy rags dying with starvation—no drugs—no food. . . . The TB allied to starvation gives the people a Belsen-like appearance. In one ward a boy of thirteen tied down to the bed because he was going insane—many children now orphans—or can't find families—and a lot of nervous twitches and spasms to be seen among the people. The face of one small boy of eighteen months was in a state of destruction by what appeared to be infected skin and flesh which had broken down under severe kwashiorkor—his eyes full of pus, held in the arms of his five-year-old sister . . . I find this sort of thing very tough to take—and this situation must be applicable to hundreds of thousands of Kampuchean people today."

Two weeks before reading these words, A. went out to din-ner with a friend of his, P., a writer and editor for a large weekly news magazine. It so happens that she was handling the "Cambodia story" for her publication. Nearly everything writ-ten in the American and foreign press about the conditions there had passed before her eyes, and she told A. about a story written for a North Carolina newspaper—by a volunteer Amer-ican doctor in one of the refugee camps across the Thai border.

It concerned the visit of the American President's wife, Ros-
alynn Carter, to those camps. A. could remember the photographs that had been published in the newspapers and
magazines (the First Lady embracing a Cambodian child, the
First Lady talking to doctors), and in spite of everything he
knew about America's responsibility for creating the conditions
Mrs. Carter had come to protest, he had been moved by those
pictures. It turned out that Mrs. Carter visited the camp where
the American doctor was working. The camp hospital was a
make-shift affair: a thatched roof, a few support beams, the patients lying on mats on the ground. The President's wife arrived,
followed by a swarm of officials, reporters, and cameramen.
There were too many of them, and as they trooped through the
hospital, patients' hands were stepped on by heavy Western
shoes, I.V. lines were disconnected by passing legs, bodies were
inadvertently kicked. Perhaps this confusion was avoidable,
perhaps not. In any case, after the visitors had completed their
inspection, the American doctor made an appeal. Please, he
said, would some of you spare a bit of your time to donate
blood to the hospital; even the blood of the healthiest Cambodian is too thin to be of use; our supply has run out. But the
First Lady's tour was behind schedule. There were other places
to go that day, other suffering people to see. There was just no
time, they said. Sorry. So very sorry. And then, as abruptly as
they had come, the visitors left.

In that the world is monstrous. In that the world can lead a man
to nothing but despair, and a despair so complete, so resolute,
that nothing can open the door of this prison, which is hope-
lessness, A. peers through the bars of his cell and finds only one
thought that brings him any consolation: the image of his son.
And not just his son, but any son, any daughter, any child of
any man or woman.

In that the world is monstrous. In that it seems to offer no
hope of a future, A. looks at his son and realizes that he must
not allow himself to despair. There is this responsibility for a
young life, and in that he has brought this life into being, he
must not despair. Minute by minute, hour by hour, as he remains

in the presence of his son, attending to his needs, giving himself up to this young life, which is a continual injunction to remain in the present, he feels his despair evaporate. And even though he continues to despair, he does not allow himself to despair.

The thought of a child's suffering, therefore, is monstrous to him. It is even more monstrous than the monstrosity of the world itself. For it robs the world of its one consolation, and in that a world can be imagined without consolation, it is monstrous.

He can go no farther than this.

This is where it begins. He stands alone in an empty room and begins to cry. "It is too much for me, I cannot face it" (Mallarmé). "A Belsen-like appearance," as the engineer in Cambodia noted. And yes, that is the place where Anne Frank died.

"It's really a wonder," she wrote, just three weeks before her arrest, "that I haven't dropped all my ideals, because they seem so absurd and impossible to carry out. . . . I see the world gradually being turned into a wilderness, I hear the ever-approaching thunder, which will destroy us too, I can feel the sufferings of millions and yet, if I look up into the heavens, I think that it will all come right, that this cruelty too will end. . . ."

No, he does not mean to say that this is the only thing. He does not even pretend to say that it can be understood, that by talking about it and talking about it a meaning can be discovered for it. No, it is not the only thing, and life nevertheless continues, for some, if not for most. And yet, in that it is a thing that will forever escape understanding, he wants it to stand for him as the thing that will always come before the beginning. As in the sentences: "This is where it begins. He stands alone in an empty room and begins to cry."

Return to the belly of the whale.

"The word of the Lord came unto Jonah . . . saying, Arise, go to Ninevah, that great city, and cry against it. . . ."

In this command as well, Jonah's story differs from that of all the other prophets. For the Ninevites are not Jews. Unlike the other carriers of God's word, Jonah is not asked to address his own people, but foreigners. Even worse, they are the enemies of his people. Ninevah was the capital of Assyria, the most power- ful empire in the world at that time. In the words of Nahum (whose prophecies have been preserved on the same scroll as the story of Jonah): "the bloody city . . . full of lies and rapine."

"Arise, go to Ninevah," God tells Jonah. Ninevah is to the east. Jonah promptly goes west, to Tarshish (Tartessus, on the farthest tip of Spain). Not only does he run away, he goes to the limit of the known world. This flight is not difficult to un- derstand. Imagine an analogous case: a Jew being told to enter Germany during the Second World War and preach against the National Socialists. It is a thought that begs the impossible.

As early as the second century, one of the rabbinical commen- tators argued that Jonah boarded the ship to drown himself in the sea for the sake of Israel, not to flee from the presence of God. This is the political reading of the book, and Christian interpreters quickly turned it against the Jews. Theodore of Mop- suestia, for example, says that Jonah was sent to Ninevah be- cause the Jews refused to listen to the prophets, and the book about Jonah was written to teach a lesson to the "stiff-necked people." Rupert of Deutz, however, another Christian interpreter (twelfth century), contends that the prophet refused God's com- mand out of piety to his people, and for this reason God did not become very angry with Jonah. This echoes the opinion of Rabbi Akiba himself, who stated that "Jonah was jealous for the glory of the son (Israel) but not for the glory of the father (God)."

Nevertheless, Jonah finally agrees to go to Ninevah. But even after he delivers his message, even after the Ninevites repent and change their ways, even after God spares them, we learn that "it displeased Jonah exceedingly, and he was very angry." This is a patriotic anger. Why should the enemies of Israel be spared? It is at this point that God teaches Jonah the lesson of the book— in the parable of the gourd that follows.

"Doest thou well to be angry?" he asks. Jonah then removes himself to the outskirts of Ninevah, "till he might see what would become of the city"—implying that he still felt there was a

chance Ninevah would be destroyed, or that he hoped the
Ninevites would revert to their sinful ways and bring down pun-
ishment on themselves. God prepares a gourd (a castor plant) to
protect Jonah from the sun, and "Jonah was exceedingly glad of
the gourd." But by the next morning God has made the plant
wither away. A vehement east wind blows, a fierce sun beats
down on Jonah, and "he fainted, and wished himself to die, and
said, it is better for me to die than to live"—the same words he
had used earlier, indicating that the message of this parable is the
same as in the first part of the book. "And God said to Jonah,
Doest thou well to be angry for the gourd? And he said, I do well
to be angry, even unto death. Then said the Lord, Thou hast had
pity on the gourd, for which thou has not labored, neither madest
it grow; which came up in a night and perished in a night; And
should I not spare Ninevah, that great city, wherein are more
than sixscore thousand persons that cannot discern between their
right hand and their left hand; and also much cattle?"

These sinners, these heathen—and even the beasts that belong
to them—are as much God's creatures as the Hebrews. This is a
startling and original notion, especially considering the date of
the story—eighth century B.C. (the time of Heraclitus). But this,
finally, is the essence of what the rabbis have to teach. If there is
to be any justice at all, it must be a justice for everyone. No one
can be excluded, or else there is no such thing as justice. The
conclusion is inescapable. This tiniest of books, which tells the
curious and even comical story of Jonah, occupies a central
place in the liturgy: it is read each year in the synagogue on
Yom Kippur, the Day of Atonement, which is the most solemn
day on the Jewish calendar. For everything, as has been noted
before, is connected to everything else. And if there is everything, then it follows there is everyone. He does not forget
Jonah's last words: "I do well to be angry, even unto death."
And still, he finds himself writing these words on the page before him. If there is everything, then it follows there is everyone.

The words rhyme, and even if there is no real connection between them, he cannot help thinking of them together. Room

and tomb, tomb and womb, womb and room. Breath and death. Or the fact that the letters of the word "live" can be rearranged to spell out the word "evil." He knows this is no more than a schoolboy's game. Surprisingly, however, as he writes the word "schoolboy," he can remember himself at eight or nine years old, and the sudden sense of power he felt in himself when he discovered he could play with words in this way—as if he had accidentally found a secret path to the truth: the absolute, universal, and unshakeable truth that lies hidden at the center of the world. In his schoolboy enthusiasm, of course, he had neglected to consider the existence of languages other than English, the great Babel of tongues buzzing and battling in the world outside his schoolboy life. And how can the absolute and unshakeable truth change from language to language?

Still, the power of rhyming words, of word transformations, cannot altogether be dismissed. The feeling of magic remains, even if it cannot be connected with a search for the truth, and this same magic, these same correspondences between words, are present in every language, even though the particular combinations are different. At the heart of each language there is a network of rhymes, assonances, and overlapping meanings, and each of these occurrences functions as a kind of bridge that joins opposite and contrasting aspects of the world with one another. Language, then, not simply as a list of separate things to be added up and whose sum total is equal to the world. Rather, language as it is laid out in the dictionary: an infinitely complex organism, all of whose elements—cells and sinews, corpuscles and bones, digits and fluids—are present in the world simultaneously, none of which can exist on its own. For each word is defined by other words, which means that to enter any part of language is to enter the whole of it. Language, then, as a monadology, to echo the term used by Leibniz. ("Since all is a plenum, all matter is connected and all movement in the plenum produces some effect on the distant bodies, in proportion to the distance. Hence every body is affected not only by those with which it is in contact, and thus feels in some way everything that happens to them; but through them it also feels those that touch the ones with which it is in immediate contact. Hence it follows that this communication extends over any distance whatever. Consequently, every body experiences everything that goes on in the universe, so much so that he who sees everything might read in any body what is happening anywhere, and even what has happened or will happen. He would be able to observe in the present what is remote in both time and space. . . . A soul, however, can read in itself only what is directly represented in it; it is unable to unfold all at once all its folds; for these go on into infinity.")

Playing with words in the way A. did as a schoolboy, then, was not so much a search for the truth as a search for the world as it appears in language. Language is not truth. It is the way we exist in the world. Playing with words is merely to examine the way the mind functions, to mirror a particle of the world as the mind perceives it. In the same way, the world is not just the sum of the things that are in it. It is the infinitely complex network of connections among them. As in the meanings of words, things take on meaning only in relationship to each other. "Two faces are alike," writes Pascal. "Neither is funny by itself, but side by side their likeness makes us laugh." The faces rhyme for the eye, just as two words can rhyme for the ear. To carry the proposition one step further, A. would contend that it is possible for events in one's life to rhyme as well. A young man rents a room in Paris and then discovers that his father had hid out in this same room during the war. If these two events were to be considered separately, there would be little to say about either one of them. The rhyme they create when looked at together alters the reality of each. Just as two physical objects, when brought into proximity of each other, give off electromagnetic forces that not only effect the molecular structure of each but the space between them as well, altering, as it were, the very environment, so it is that two (or more) rhyming events set up a connection in the world, adding one more synapse to be routed through the vast plenum of experience.

These connections are commonplace in literary works (to return to that argument), but one tends not to see them in the world—for the world is too big and one's life is too small. It is only at those rare moments when one happens to glimpse a rhyme in the world that the mind can leap out of itself and serve as a bridge for things across time and space, across seeing and memory. But there is more to it than just rhyme. The grammar of existence includes all the figures of language itself: simile, metaphor, metonymy, synecdoche—so that each thing encountered in the world is actually many things, which in turn give way to many other things, depending on what these things are next to, contained by, or removed from. Often, too, the second term of a comparison is missing. It can be forgotten, or buried in the unconscious, or somehow made unavailable. "The past is hidden," Proust writes in an important passage of his novel, "beyond the reach of intellect, in some material object (in the sensation which that material object will give us) which we do not suspect. And as for that object, it depends on chance whether we come upon it or not before we ourselves must die." Everyone has experienced in one way or another the strange sensations of forgetfulness, the mystifying force of the missing term. I walked into that room, a man will say, and the oddest feeling came over me, as if I had been there before, although I cannot remember it at all. As in Pavlov's experiments with dogs (which, at the simplest possible level, demonstrate the way in which the mind can make a connection between two dissimilar things, eventually forget the first thing, and thereby turn one thing into another thing), something has happened, although we are at a loss to say what it is. What A. is struggling to express, perhaps, is that for some time now none of the terms has been missing for him. Wherever his eye or mind seems to stop, he discovers another connection, another bridge to carry him to yet another place, and even in the solitude of his room, the world has been rushing in on him at a dizzying speed, as if it were all suddenly converging in him and happening to him at once. Coincidence: to fall on with; to occupy the same place in time or space. The mind, therefore, as that which contains more than itself. As in the phrase from Augustine: "But where is the part of it which it does not itself contain?"

Second return to the belly of the whale.

   "When he recovered his senses the Marionette could not remember where he was. Around him all was darkness, a darkness so deep and so black that for a moment he thought he had been dipped head first into an inkwell."

This is Collodi's description of Pinocchio's arrival in the belly of the shark. It would have been one thing to write it in the ordinary way: "a darkness as black as ink"—as a trite literary flourish to be forgotten the moment it is read. But something different is happening here, something that transcends the question of good or bad writing (and this is manifestly not bad writing). Take careful note: Collodi makes no comparisons in this passage; there is no "as if," no "like," nothing to equate or contrast one thing with another. The image of absolute darkness immediately gives way to an image of an inkwell. Pinocchio has just entered the belly of the shark. He does not know yet that Gepetto is also there. Everything, at least for this brief moment, has been lost. Pinocchio is surrounded by the darkness of solitude. And it is in this darkness, where the puppet will eventually find the courage to save his father and thereby bring about his transformation into a real boy, that the essential creative act of the book takes place.

By plunging his marionette into the darkness of the shark, Collodi is telling us, he is dipping his pen into the darkness of his inkwell. Pinocchio, after all, is only made of wood. Collodi is using him as the instrument (literally, the pen) to write the story of himself. This is not to indulge in primitive psychologizing. Collodi could not have achieved what he does in *Pinocchio* unless the book was for him a book of memory. He was over fifty years old when he sat down to write it, recently retired from an undistinguished career in government service, which had been marked, according to his nephew, "neither by zeal nor by punctuality nor by subordination." No less than Proust's novel in search of lost time, his story is a search for his lost childhood. Even the name he chose to write under was an evocation of the past. His real name was Carlo Lorenzini. Collodi was the name of the small town where his mother had been born and where he spent his holidays as a young child. About this childhood, a few facts are available. He was a teller of tall tales, admired by his friends for his ability to fascinate them with stories. According to his brother Ippolito, "He did it so well and with such mimickry that half the world took delight and the children listened to him with their mouths agape." In an autobiographical sketch written late in life, long after the completion of *Pinocchio*, Collodi leaves little doubt that he conceived of himself as the puppet's double. He portrays himself as a prankster and a clown—eating cherries in class and stuffing the pits into a schoolmate's pockets, catching flies and putting them into someone else's ears, painting figures on the clothes of the boy in front of him: in general, creating havoc for everyone. Whether or not this is true is beside the point. Pinocchio was Collodi's surrogate, and after the puppet had been created, Collodi saw himself as Pinocchio. The puppet had become the image of himself as a child. To dip the puppet into the inkwell, therefore, was to use his creation to write the story of himself. For it is only in the darkness of solitude that the work of memory begins.

Possible epigraph(s) for The Book of Memory.

"We ought surely to look in the child for the first traces of imaginative activity. The child's best loved and most absorbing occupation is play. Perhaps we may say that every child at play behaves like an imaginative writer, in that he creates a world of his own or, more truly, he rearranges the things of his world and orders it in a new way. . . . It would be incorrect to think that he does not take this world seriously; on the contrary, he takes his play very seriously and expends a great deal of emotion on it." (Freud)

"You will not forget that the stress laid on the writer's memories of his childhood, which perhaps seem so strange, is ultimately derived from the hypothesis that imaginative creation, like day dreaming, is a continuation of and substitute for the play of childhood." (Freud)

He watches his son. He watches the little boy move around the room and listens to what he says. He sees him playing with his toys and hears him talking to himself. Each time the boy picks up an object, or pushes a truck across the floor, or adds another block to the tower of blocks growing before him, he speaks of what he is doing, in the same way a narrator in a film would speak, or else he makes up a story to accompany the actions he has set in motion. Each movement engenders a word, or a series of words; each word triggers off another movement: a reversal, a continuation, a new set of movements and words. There is no fixed center to any of this ("a universe in which the center is everywhere, the circumference nowhere") except perhaps the child's consciousness, which is itself a constantly shifting field of perceptions, memories, and utterances. There is no law of nature that cannot be broken: trucks fly, a block becomes a person, the dead are resurrected at will. From one thing, the child's mind careens without hesitation to another thing. Look, he says, my broccoli is a tree. Look, my potatoes are a cloud. Look at the cloud, it's a man. Or else, feeling the food as it touches his tongue, and looking up, with a sly glint in his eyes: "Do you know how Pinocchio and his father escape from the shark?" Pause, letting the question sink in. Then, in a whisper: "They tiptoe quietly over his tongue."

It sometimes seems to A. that his son's mental perambulations while at play are an exact image of his own progress through the labyrinth of his book. He has even thought that if he could somehow make a diagram of his son at play (an exhaustive description, containing every shift, association, and gesture) and then make a similar diagram of his book (elaborating what takes place in the gaps between words, the interstices of the syntax, the blanks between sections—in other words, unraveling the spool of connections), the two diagrams would be the same: the one would fit perfectly over the other.

During the time he has worked on The Book of Memory, it has given him special pleasure to watch the boy remember. Like all preliterate beings, the boy's memory is astonishing. The capacity for detailed observation, for seeing an object in its singularity, is almost boundless. Written language absolves one of the need to remember much of the world, for the memories are stored in the words. The child, however, standing in a place before the advent of the written word, remembers in the same way Cicero would recommend, in the same way devised by any number of classical writers on the subject: image wed to place. One day, for example (and this is only one example, plucked from a myriad of possibilities), A. and his son were walking down the street. They ran into a nursery school playmate of the boy's standing outside a pizza parlor with his father. A.'s son was delighted to see his friend, but the other boy seemed to shy away from the encounter. Say hello, Kenny, his father urged him, and the boy managed to summon forth a feeble greeting. Then A. and his son continued on their walk. Three or four months later, they happened to be walking past the same spot together. A. suddenly heard his son muttering to himself, in a barely audible voice: Say hello, Kenny, say hello. It occurred to A. that if in some sense the world imprints itself on our minds, it is equally true that our experiences are imprinted on the world. For that brief moment, as they walked by the pizza parlor, the boy was literally seeing his own past. The past, to repeat the words of Proust, is hidden in some material object. To wander about in the world, then, is also to wander about in ourselves. That is to say, the moment we step into the space of memory, we walk into the world.

It is a lost world. And it strikes him to realize that it will be lost forever. The boy will forget everything that has happened to him so far. There will be nothing left but a kind of after-glow, and perhaps not even that. All the thousands of hours that A. has spent with him during the first three years of his life, all the millions of words he has spoken to him, the books he has read to him, the meals he has made for him, the tears he has wiped for him—all these things will vanish from the boy's memory forever.

The Book of Memory. Book Thirteen.
    He remembers that he gave himself a new name, John, because all cowboys were named John, and that each time his mother addressed him by his real name he would refuse to answer her. He remembers running out of the house and lying in the middle of the road with his eyes shut, waiting for a car to run him over. He remembers that his grandfather gave him a large photograph of Gabby Hayes and that it sat in a place of honor on the top of his bureau. He remembers thinking the

world was flat. He remembers learning how to tie his shoes. He remembers that his father's clothes were kept in the closet in his room and that it was the noise of hangers clicking together in the morning that would wake him up. He remembers the sight of his father knotting his tie and saying to him, Rise and shine little boy. He remembers wanting to be a squirrel, because he wanted to be light like a squirrel and have a bushy tail and be able to jump from tree to tree as though he were flying. He remembers looking through the venetian blinds and seeing his newborn sister coming home from the hospital in his mother's arms. He remembers the nurse in a white dress who sat beside his baby sister and gave him little squares of Swiss chocolate. He remembers that she called them Swiss although he did not know what that meant. He remembers lying in his bed at dusk in midsummer and looking at the tree through his window and seeing different faces in the configuration of the branches. He remembers sitting in the bathtub and pretending that his knees were mountains and that the white soap was an ocean liner. He remembers the day his father gave him a plum and told him to go outside and ride his tricycle. He remembers that he did not like the taste of the plum and that he threw it into the gutter and was overcome by a feeling of guilt. He remembers the day his mother took him and his friend B. to the television studio in Newark to see a showing of Junior Frolics. He remembers that Uncle Fred had makeup on his face, just like his mother wore, and that he was surprised by this. He remembers that the cartoons were shown on a little television set, no bigger than the one at home, and the disappointment he felt was so crushing that he wanted to stand up and shout his protests to Uncle Fred. He remembers that he had been expecting to see Farmer Gray and Felix the Cat run around on a stage, as large as life, going at each other with real pitchforks and rakes. He remembers that B.'s favorite color was green and that he claimed his teddy bear had green blood running through its veins. He remembers that B. lived with both his grandmothers and that to get to B.'s room you had to go through an upstairs sitting room where the two white-haired women spent all their time watching television. He remembers that he and B. would go scavenging through the bushes and backyards of the neighborhood looking for dead animals. He remembers burying them by the side of his house, deep in the darkness of the ivy, and that mostly they were birds, little birds like sparrows and robins and wrens. He remembers building crosses for them out of twigs and saying a prayer over their bodies as he and B. laid them in the hole they had dug in the ground, the dead eyes touching the loose damp earth. He remembers taking apart the family radio one afternoon with a hammer and screwdriver and explaining to his mother that he had done it as a scientific experiment. He remembers these were the words he used and that his mother spanked him. He remembers trying to chop down a small fruit tree in the back yard with a dull axe he had found in the garage and managing to make no more than a few dents in it. He remembers seeing the green on the underside of the bark and getting spanked for that too. He remembers sitting at his desk in the first grade away from the other children because he had been punished for talking in class. He remembers sitting at that desk and reading a book with a red cover and red illustrations with green-blue backgrounds. He remembers the teacher coming up to him from behind and very gently putting her hand on his shoulder and whispering a question into his ear. He remembers that she was wearing a white sleeveless blouse and that her arms were thick and covered with freckles. He remembers colliding with another boy during a softball game in the schoolyard and being thrown to the ground so violently that for the next five or ten minutes he saw everything as in a photographic negative. He remembers getting to his feet and walking toward the school building and thinking to himself, I'm going blind. He remembers how his panic gradually turned to acceptance and even fascination in the space of those few minutes and how, when his normal sight returned to him, he had the feeling that some extraordinary thing had taken place inside him. He remembers wetting his bed long after it was an acceptable thing to do and the icy sheets when he woke up in the morning. He remembers being invited for the first time to sleep over at a friend's house and how he stayed awake all night for fear of wetting the bed and humiliating himself, staring at the luminescent green hands of the watch he had been given for his sixth birthday. He remembers studying the illustrations in a children's Bible and accepting the fact that God had a long white beard. He remembers thinking that the voice he heard inside himself was the voice of God. He remembers going to the circus at Madison Square Garden with his grandfather and taking a ring off the finger of an eight and a half foot giant at the sideshow for fifty cents. He remembers keeping the ring on the top of his bureau beside the photograph of Gabby Hayes and that he could put four of his fingers through it. He remembers speculating that perhaps the entire world was enclosed in a glass jar and that it sat on a shelf next to dozens of other jar-worlds in the pantry of a giant's house. He remembers refusing to sing Christmas carols at school because he was Jewish and staying behind in the classroom while the other children went to rehearse in the auditorium. He remembers coming home from the first day of Hebrew school wearing a new suit and being pushed into a creek by older boys in leather jackets who called him a Jew shit. He remembers writing his first book, a detective story he composed with green ink. He remembers thinking that if Adam and Eve were the first people in the world, then everyone was related to everyone else. He remembers wanting to throw a penny out the window of his grandparents' apartment on Columbus Circle and his grandmother telling him that it would go straight through someone's head. He remembers looking down from the top of the Empire State Building and being surprised that the taxicabs were still yellow. He remembers visiting the Statue of Liberty with his mother and remembers that she got very nervous inside the torch and made him go back down the stairs sitting, one step at a time. He remembers the boy who was killed by lightning on a hike at summer camp. He remembers lying there in the rain next to him and seeing the boy's lips turn blue. He remembers his grandmother telling him how she remembered coming to America from Russia when she was five years old. He remembers that she told him she remembered waking up from a deep sleep and finding herself in the arms of a soldier who was carrying her onto a ship.

He remembers that she told him this was the only thing she could remember.

The Book of Memory. Later that evening.

Not long after writing the words, "this was the only thing she could remember," A. stood up from his table and left his room. Walking along the street, feeling drained by his efforts that day, he decided to go on walking for a while. Darkness came. He stopped for supper, spread out a newspaper on the table before him, and then, after paying his bill, decided to spend the rest of the evening at the movies. It took him nearly an hour to walk to the theater. As he was about to buy his ticket, he changed his mind, put the money back in his pocket, and walked away. He retraced his steps, following the same route that had taken him there in reverse. At some point along the way he stopped to drink a glass of beer. Then he continued on his walk. It was nearly twelve when he opened the door of his room.

That night, for the first time in his life, he dreamed that he was dead. Twice he woke up during the dream, trembling with panic. Each time, he tried to calm himself down, told himself that by changing position in bed the dream would end, and each time, upon falling back to sleep, the dream started up again at precisely the spot it had left off.

It was not exactly that he was dead, but that he was going to die. This was certain, an absolute and immanent fact. He was lying in a hospital bed, suffering from a fatal disease. His hair had fallen out in patches, and his head was half bald. Two nurses dressed in white walked into the room and told him: "Today you are going to die. It's too late to help you." They were almost mechanical in their indifference to him. He cried and pleaded with them, "I'm too young to die, I don't want to die now." "It's too late," the nurses answered. "We have to shave your head now." With tears pouring from his eyes, he allowed them to shave his head. Then they said: "The coffin is over there. Just go and lie down in it, close your eyes, and soon you'll be dead." He wanted to run away. But he knew that it was not permitted to disobey their orders. He went over to the coffin and climbed into it. The lid was closed over him, but once inside he kept his eyes open.

Then he woke up for the first time.

After he went back to sleep, he was climbing out of the coffin. He was dressed in a white patient's gown and had no shoes on. He left the room, wandered for a long time through many corridors, and then walked out of the hospital. Soon afterwards, he was knocking on the door of his ex-wife's house. "I have to die today," he told her, "there's nothing I can do about it." She took this news calmly, acting much as the nurses had. But he was not there for her sympathy. He wanted to give her instructions about what to do with his manuscripts. He went through a long list of his writings and told her how and where to have each of them published. Then he said: "The Book of Memory isn't finished yet. There's nothing I can do about it. There won't be time to finish. You finish it for me and then give it to Daniel. I trust you. You finish it for me." She agreed to do this, but without much enthusiasm. And then he began to cry, just as he had before: "I'm too young to die. I don't want to die now." But she patiently explained to him that if it had to be, then he should accept it. Then he left her house and returned to the hospital. When he reached the parking lot, he woke up for the second time.

After he went back to sleep, he was inside the hospital again, in a basement room next to the morgue. The room was large, bare, and white, a kind of old-fashioned kitchen. A group of his childhood friends, now grownups, were sitting around a table eating a large and sumptuous meal. They all turned and stared at him when he entered the room. He explained to them: "Look, they've shaved my head. I have to die today, and I don't want to die." His friends were moved by this. They invited him to sit down and eat with them. "No," he said, "I can't eat with you. I have to go into the next room and die." He pointed to a white swinging door with a circular window in it. His friends stood up from their chairs and joined him by the door. For a little while they all reminisced about their childhood together. It soothed him to talk to them, but at the same time he found it all the more difficult to summon the courage to walk through the door. Finally, he announced: "I have to go now. I have to die now." One by one, with tears pouring down his cheeks, he embraced his friends, squeezing them with all his strength, and said good-bye.

Then he woke up for the last time.

Concluding sentences for The Book of Memory.

From a letter by Nadezhda Mandelstam to Osip Mandelstam, dated 10/22/38, and never sent.

"I have no words, my darling, to write this letter . . . I am writing it into empty space. Perhaps you will come back and not find me here. Then this will be all you have left to remember me by. . . . Life can last so long. How hard and long for each of us to die alone. Can this fate be for us who are inseparable? Puppies and children, did we deserve this? Did you deserve this, my angel? Everything goes on as before. I know nothing. Yet I know everything—each day and hour of your life are plain and clear to me as in a delirium—In my last dream I was buying food for you in a filthy hotel restaurant. The people with me were total strangers. When I had bought it, I realized I did not know where to take it, because I do not know where you are. . . . When I woke up, I said to Shura: 'Osia is dead.' I do not know whether you are still alive, but from the time of that dream, I have lost track of you. I do not know where you are. Will you hear me? Do you know how much I love you? I could never tell you how much I love you. I cannot tell you even now. I speak to you, only to you. You are with me always, and I who was such a wild and angry one and never learned to weep simple tears—now I weep and weep and weep . . . It's me: Nadia Where are you?"

He lays out a piece of blank paper on the table before him and writes these words with his pen.

The sky is blue and black and gray and yellow. The sky is not there, and it is red. All this was yesterday. All this was a hundred years ago. The sky is white. It smells of the earth, and it is not there. The sky is white like the earth, and it smells of yesterday. All this was tomorrow. All this was a hundred years from now. The sky is lemon and rose and lavender. The sky is the earth. The sky is white, and it is not there.

He wakes up. He walks back and forth between the table and the window. He sits down. He stands up. He walks back and forth between the bed and the chair. He lies down. He stares at the ceiling. He closes his eyes. He opens his eyes. He walks back and forth between the table and the window.

He finds a fresh sheet of paper. He lays it out on the table before him and writes these words with his pen.

It was. It will never be again. Remember.

1980–1981

References

(Sources of quotations not mentioned in text)

page 81   "Israel Lichtenstein's Last Testament." In *A Holocaust Reader*, edited by Lucy S. Dawidowicz. Behrman House. New York, 1976.

page 85   Flaubert. *The Letters of Gustave Flaubert*, selected, edited, and translated by Francis Steegmuller. Harvard University Press. Cambridge, 1979.

page 93   Marina Tsvetayeva. Quotations of translations by Elaine Feinstein. In *Marina Tsvetayeva: Selected Poems*. Oxford University Press, 1971.

page 93   Gregory I. Altschuller, M.D. *Marina Tsvetayeva: A Physician's Memoir*. In SUN. Volume IV, Number 3: Winter, 1980. New York.

page 95   Christopher Wright. In *Rembrandt and His Art*. Galahad Books. New York, 1975.

page 96   Hölderlin. Prose quotations translated by Michael Hamburger. In *Friedrich Hölderlin: Poems and Fragments*. University of Michigan Press. Ann Arbor, 1966.

page 97   Hölderlin. *To Zimmer*. Translated by John Riley and Tim Longville. In *What I Own: Versions of Hölderlin*. Grosseteste Review Press, 1973.

page 127   B. = André du Bouchet. In *Hölderlin Aujourd'hui*, a lecture delivered in Stuttgart, 1970.

page 130   Collodi. *The Adventures of Pinocchio*. Translated by Carol Della Chiesa. Macmillan. New York, 1925. All further quotations from this edition. Translations sometimes slightly adapted.

page 139   Edward A. Snow. *A Study of Vermeer*. University of California Press. Berkeley, 1979.

page 141   Van Gogh. *The Letters of Vincent Van Gogh*. Edited by Mark Roskill. Atheneum. New York, 1972.

page 146   Tolstoy. Ann Dunnigan's translation of *War and Peace*.
             New American Library. New York, 1968.

page 148   Freud. "The Uncanny." In *On Creativity and the Uncon-
             scious*. Harper and Row. New York, 1958.

page 149   *The Thousand and One Nights*. All quotations from *The
             Portable Arabian Nights*. Translated by John Payne. Edited
             by Joseph Campbell. Viking. New York, 1952.

page 154   Dostoyevsky. *The Brothers Karamazov*. Translated by
             David Magarshack. Penguin. Baltimore, 1958.

page 155   Jim Harrison. Quoted in "The End of Cambodia?" by
             William Shawcross. *The New York Review of Books*. Jan-
             uary 24, 1980.

page 157   Anne Frank, *The Diary of a Young Girl*. Doubleday. New
             York, 1952.

page 158   Quotations of commentaries on the Book of Jonah from
             "Jonah, or the Unfulfilled Prophecy" in *Four Strange Books
             of the Bible*, by Elias Bickerman. Schocken. New York,
             1967.

page 160   Leibniz. In *Monadology and Other Philosophical Essays*.
             Translated by Paul Schrecker and Anne Martin Schrecker.
             Bobbs-Merrill. Indianapolis, 1965.

page 162   Proust. *Swann's Way*. Translated by C.K. Scott Moncrieff.
             Random House. New York, 1928.

page 164   Freud. "The Relation of the Poet to Day-Dreaming." In
             On Creativity and the Unconscious.

page 172   Nadezhda Mandelstam. *Hope Abandoned*. Translated by
             Max Hayward. Collins & Harvill. London, 1974.